THE POPULIST PARADOX

THE POPULIST PARADOX

INTEREST GROUP INFLUENCE AND

THE PROMISE OF DIRECT LEGISLATION

Elisabeth R. Gerber

PRINCETON UNIVERSITY PRESS   PRINCETON, NEW JERSEY

Library of Congress Cataloging-in-Publication Data

Gerber, Elisabeth R., 1964–
The populist paradox : interest group influence and the
promise of direct legislation / Elisabeth R. Gerber.
p.   cm.
Includes bibliographical references.
ISBN 0-691-00266-5 (cloth : alk. paper)
ISBN 0-691-00267-3 (pbk. : alk. paper)
1. Referendum—United States.   2. Pressure groups—
United States.   I. Title.
JF494.G47   1999
324′.4′0973—dc21   98-54178   CIP

This book has been composed in Times Roman

The paper used in this publication meets the minimum requirements
of ANSI/NISO Z39.48-1992 (R1997) (*Permanence of Paper*)

http://pup.princeton.edu

Printed in the United States of America

10 9 8 7 6 5 4 3 2 1

10 9 8 7 6 5 4 3 2 1
(Pbk.)

To Skip and Francesca

_____

Contents

Figures

Tables

Acknowledgments ⎯⎯⎯⎯⎯⎯⎯⎯⎯⎯⎯⎯⎯⎯⎯⎯

IN THE COURSE of writing this book, I have incurred many debts of gratitude. Skip Lupia and Bruce Cain each read several drafts of the entire manuscript and fundamentally influenced how I think about the problem of interest group influence. Numerous individuals provided invaluable comments and suggestions at various stages of this project including Mat McCubbins, Sam Popkin, Becky Morton, Simon Hug, Frank Baumgartner, Dan Smith, David Radwin, Michael Molloy, John Ellwood, Scott Gartner, several anonymous reviewers, and seminar participants at the University of California, San Diego; the University of California, Los Angeles; New York University; Columbia University; the Public Policy Institute of California; the Hoover Institution; and the Institute of Governmental Studies. I am indebted to my colleagues at UCSD for cultivating a productive work environment. I also thank Christopher den Hartog, Tim Groeling, Michael Holman, Jennifer Kuhn, Daniel Murdock, Neelima Shan, Gina Simas, and Amanda Smith for their diligent research assistance.

This research reflects the strong influence of Jack Walker on my intellectual development. I am fortunate to have been his student.

Finally, I thank my family, especially my parents, for their confidence, encouragement, and unconditional support.

THE POPULIST PARADOX

1

What Is the Populist Paradox?

> Among the difficulties encountered by the
> [Constitutional] convention, a very important one
> must have lain in combining the requisite stability
> and energy in government with the inviolable
> attention due to liberty and to the republican form.
> —James Madison, *The Federalist Papers*

ALL DEMOCRACIES face a fundamental problem in deciding how much political participation to allow and by whom. As Madison noted, perhaps the most
fundamental trade-off in designing democratic government rests between limiting participation to ensure "stability and energy in government" and expanding participation to promote liberty. Disagreement over the proper balance
between limiting and expanding participation was at the root of some of the
most famous debates of the constitutional period.[1] It continues to this day.

To Madison, the greatest threat to a democracy was the destabilizing potential of broad participation in government. He argued that "measures are too
often decided, not according to the rules of justice and the rights of the minor
party, but by the superior force of an interested and overbearing majority"
(James Madison in Hamilton et al. 1961, p. 77). To mitigate the destabilizing
potential of mass participation, and to protect minority interests, Madison advocated checks, balances, and a representative form of government.

All across America, and at all levels of government, the institutionalization
of Madisonian ideals limited the power of the majority. In fact, these limits
were so effective that over the past two hundred years, citizens have periodically felt it necessary to counteract excessive minority control. Perhaps
the most important such attempt occurred at the dawn of the twentieth century. At that time, activists in many American states advocated direct legislation as a way to dilute the increasing power of narrow industry-based interest
groups.

Direct legislation is policy making at the ballot box. The two types of direct
legislation are *initiatives* (laws initiated by citizens and then put to a popular
vote) and *referendums* (laws initiated by the legislature and then ratified or

---

[1] Perhaps the most noted participants in this debate were Madison, who advocated limited
citizen participation, and Jefferson, who championed greater participation (see Elkins and
McKitrick 1993).

rejected by voters).[2] Direct legislation's early advocates argued that allowing citizens to make policy would shift the balance of power from narrow economic interests to broader-based concerns. These early advocates emerged from and embodied several different reform movements.

In the late nineteenth century, the Populists mobilized in reaction to rapid industrialization and consequent economic dislocation. The Populists argued for a simpler, nonindustrial way of life, promoting laws that benefited agrarian and nonindustrial interests such as public ownership of the railroads and a graduated income tax. The Populists claimed that because the major political parties were beholden to corporate interests, they would block any attempt to reverse the effects of industrialization. To circumvent the parties, the Populists advocated direct legislation as a way to empower "plain people" to pass these policies.[3]

A decade or so later, the Progressive movement emerged in the American West and Midwest. Like the Populists, the Progressives were concerned about the increasing political power of concentrated wealth. They claimed that corporate money in politics corrupted politicians, parties, and the political process. They advocated direct legislation as a way to neutralize corruption and to pass laws that promoted middle-class values.[4]

Although the Progressive goal of reducing corruption differed significantly from the Populist goal of returning to a simpler way of life, reformers from both movements were motivated by a common belief that narrow economic interests made state legislatures unresponsive to broader interests. Both saw the promise of direct legislation as providing citizens with a means for regaining control of the legislative process.[5] Since its inception, however, many observers have questioned whether this promise has been met. Contemporary observers argue that just as wealthy interests manipulated state legislatures early in this century, their modern counterparts manipulate direct legislation today (see, e.g., California Commission on Campaign Financing 1992).

The evidence most often offered in support of these claims is the enormous level of spending in direct legislation campaigns. In the 1988 Cali-

---

[2] There are also two versions of initiatives (direct and indirect) and two versions of referendums (popular and submitted). I describe each of these in detail below.

[3] See Cronin (1989) for a thorough description of Populists and Progressive involvement in the adoption of direct legislation.

[4] Deverell and Sitton (1994) argued that the Progressive movement actually encompassed several groups with distinct interests and issue agendas, ranging from the defense of middle-class economic interests to concerns about good government to moral issues. Each of these constituent groups believed that industrial interests' control of the political parties and state legislatures impeded progress toward their reform goals.

[5] The motives of the Populist and Progressive movements continue to be debated. One revisionist view is that the movements simply represented coalitions of special interests—the Populists representing farming interests and the Progressives representing middle-class interests—and not citizens more broadly. However, viewing these movements as coalitions of the economically dislocated or disadvantaged interests in society (as with the Populists) or of the middle class (as with the Progressives) is not inconsistent with the notion that direct legislation was adopted to mitigate the power of large economic or industrial interests.

fornia general election, for example, supporters and opponents of the twenty-nine statewide ballot propositions spent over $129 million to promote their causes (California Fair Political Practices Commission 1988b). Critics were outraged, calling the level of spending "obscene" and "scandalous."[6] But the 1988 election was no anomaly. Viewed from a longer time perspective, we see that 1988 reflected the continuation of a spending trend that began in the late 1970s. In 1976, proponents and opponents spent approximately $9 million on statewide initiative campaigns in California (California Commission on Campaign Financing 1992). By 1986, this figure grew to $34 million. Spending peaked in 1988 and 1990, with $127 million and $110 million spent, respectively. Although spending on initiative campaigns has dropped off to some extent since 1990, it continues well above its pre-1988 levels. Spending in other states has reached staggering levels as well. Proponents and opponents spent more than $15 million in the campaigns for and against Washington's twelve initiatives between 1990 and 1994 (Washington Secretary of State 1990–1994). Average per-measure spending on Michigan's four statewide initiatives in 1992 was more than $5 million (Michigan Secretary of State 1992).

These expensive campaigns have led some critics to suspect that wealthy interests are using direct legislation to buy favorable policy at the ballot box. They fear that, despite the efforts of the Populist and Progressive reformers, the balance between citizen and economic interests has shifted too far in the direction of the economic interests. According to this view, direct legislation has paradoxically become a powerful instrument of wealthy interest groups rather than a popular balance against these groups. As Larry Berg and Craig Holman wrote, "the initiative process tends to become an instrument of the same special interests it was originally intended to control" (quoted in *Los Angeles Times* 1988). And as pollster Mervin Field exclaimed after the 1994 election, "The initiative process is now at odds with its original purpose—the special interests have taken over" (Roberts 1994). From this perspective, the *populist paradox*—the alleged transformation of direct legislation from a tool of regular citizens to a tool of special interests—undermines the promise of popular policy making at the ballot box.

But something is missing in these accounts of gloom and doom. Besides journalistic speculation and some colorful anecdotes, there is little systematic evidence about the relationship between money and interest group power in the direct legislation process. As a result, many important questions remain unanswered.

- Can wealthy interest groups use direct legislation to affect public policy?
- What factors enhance or inhibit their influence?

---

[6] These remarks were made by State Controller Gray Davis and State Attorney General John K. Van de Kamp, respectively, supporters of two of the 1988 insurance propositions (Shuit and Reich 1988).

- Can narrow economic interest groups use direct legislation to pass laws that are detrimental to broader interests?
- Can the involvement of wealthy interests have favorable consequences?
- Finally, is the populist paradox reality or illusion?

The purpose of this book is to answer these questions by studying the role and influence of interest groups in the direct legislation process. Such a study is needed because the populist paradox is, at its core, the belief that economic interest groups use direct legislation to the detriment of other interests. To determine the extent to which this belief is valid, it is therefore necessary to understand how interest groups, particularly economic interest groups, can and cannot use direct legislation to influence policy.

A critical part of my argument is that it is a mistake to equate money with influence in the context of direct legislation. Without a doubt, organized interests, especially business interests, now play a greater financial role in the direct legislation process than at any other time in history. Big spending, however, does not necessarily imply big influence. To pass initiatives and referendums, interest groups must be able to mobilize an electoral majority. As wealthy interests such as the insurance industry, trial lawyer associations, and tobacco companies have recently learned after expensive defeats at the ballot box, if voters do not like what initiative proponents are selling, not even vast amounts of campaign spending can get them to vote for a new policy. This is not to say that money is irrelevant in the direct legislation process. Rather, my argument is that the relationship between money and influence is far more complex and more limited than many observers believe.

In the following section, I outline a theory of interest group influence. The theory is based on five simple premises that clarify the relationship between money and influence in the direct legislation process. From these premises, I deduce a set of conclusions about how and when interest groups can use direct legislation to influence policy. The main conclusion I derive is that, contrary to popular opinion, economic groups generally do not possess the resources to overcome some of the most important hurdles to success in the direct legislation arena. I conclude that economic interest groups are therefore severely constrained in their ability to use direct legislation to the detriment of broader interests.

A Theory of Interest Group Influence

Premises

My theory is built on five basic concepts or premises. My first premise (explored in depth in chapter 2) is that groups choose between numerous possible forms of influence and specific direct legislation strategies. I assume that interest groups in the direct legislation process are analogous to profit-maximizing firms as they are characterized in microeconomics. Like firms, interest groups have the goal of changing an outcome (i.e., influencing policy). Like firms, they can achieve their goal in several ways (i.e., they can choose from among different political strategies). And like firms, an interest group's resources determine which political strategies it can afford to pursue and whether the interest group achieves its goal.

The profit-maximizing firm analogy is useful because it emphasizes the constrained maximization problem that both interest groups and profit-maximizing firms confront. Interest groups attempt to maximize their political influence by choosing between alternative political strategies and forms of influence. Firms attempt to maximize profits by choosing between alternative modes of production. Both interest groups and firms evaluate the expected costs and benefits of alternative courses of action and choose those that promise the greatest net benefits. As with firms, uncertainty and limited resources restrict a group's ability to identify and pursue an optimal political strategy.

Differences between firms also help to highlight differences between interest groups. For example, some firms have a comparative advantage at raising capital, whereas others have a comparative advantage in mobilizing labor. These respective advantages should influence a firm's decisions about how to conduct its business. For example, firms that can raise money are more likely to benefit from involvement in capital-intensive activities. Interest groups differ in analogous ways. Economic-based interest groups have a comparative advantage at raising the funds required to buy television time, contribute to campaigns, and hire consultants. Broad-based citizen groups, by contrast, may have a comparative advantage in motivating the political equivalent of labor: voters and, ultimately, electoral support. These respective advantages should affect interest group decisions about how to influence policy.

My second premise (chap. 2) is that interest groups use direct legislation to achieve one of four forms of influence. Groups may attempt either to modify the status quo (i.e., replace the existing policy with a new one) or to preserve the status quo (i.e., protect existing policy from someone else's attempt to change it). Groups may modify or protect the status quo either directly, by prevailing at the ballot box, or indirectly, by pressuring other actors to modify or preserve policy for them. In sum, the combination of these two components results in four forms of influence: direct modifying, direct preserving, indirect modifying, and indirect preserving.

My third premise (chap. 3) is that institutions and the behavior of other actors create hurdles that groups must clear if they hope to influence policy. Examples of these hurdles include drafting a measure, qualifying a measure for the ballot, and running a winning campaign. To achieve a given form of influence, groups choose strategies that involve overcoming some or all of these hurdles. Strategies for changing the status quo include proposing an initiative, forming a committee to campaign in favor of an initiative proposition, contributing money or volunteers to an existing campaign committee, and publicly endorsing an initiative. Strategies for preserving the status quo include proposing a referendum to negate legislation the group opposes, proposing a "killer" initiative to prevent passage of an unfavorable measure already on the ballot, forming a committee to campaign against an initiative, and contributing money or volunteers to an existing committee opposing an initiative.

My fourth premise (chap. 4) is that groups need particular resources to clear the hurdles associated with a given strategy. These resources include monetary resources such as cash and other financial assets and personnel resources such as members, volunteers, and experts. Different strategies require different resources. To overcome the hurdles associated with some direct legislation strategies, groups must expend monetary resources. To overcome the hurdles associated with other direct legislation strategies, groups must expend personnel resources, whereas to overcome the hurdles associated with still other strategies, groups can employ either monetary or personnel resources. The type and amount of resources a group requires to achieve influence depends on the form of influence it seeks to achieve and its relationship with other policy actors (especially voters and state legislators).

My fifth premise (chap. 4) is that groups have comparative advantages in mobilizing the different resources required by direct legislation strategies. A group's ability to mobilize monetary and personnel resources depends largely on its membership composition. Groups whose members are primarily firms and organizational representatives can more easily mobilize monetary resources, whereas groups whose members are primarily autonomous individuals can more easily mobilize personnel resources. A group's resources will affect the strategies it can choose, the difficulty of clearing the hurdles associated with those strategies, and, as a result, the forms of influence it can have.

Conclusions

My premises generate a set of conclusions about interest group strategies and influence. If citizen and economic interest groups have the comparative advantages described above, then I expect to observe the following patterns between group resources and strategies. Because citizen groups tend to have the personnel resources required to mobilize broad-based electoral support, they are better able to amass an electoral majority. When they have sufficient capital to participate at all, I therefore expect citizen groups to employ strategies aimed at proposing and passing new initiatives. Economic interest groups, by contrast, should anticipate a more difficult time using their resources to achieve victory at the ballot box and should instead pursue largely defensive or indirect strategies. Analyzing surveys of interest group activities and motivations, as well as campaign finance data from 161 initiative and referendum campaigns in eight states, I find strong empirical evidence in support of these theoretical conclusions. Citizen groups report using the direct legislation process to pass new laws and contribute to campaigns to support new initiative legislation. Economic groups report using the direct legislation process to pressure the legislature and direct a large share of their financial resources to opposition campaigns. I present these empirical results in chapter 5.

I expect these patterns of interest group behavior to translate into patterns of policy outcomes. Specifically, I expect the laws that pass by initiative to reflect the interests of citizen groups that use the process to achieve direct modifying influence. I expect the laws that fail to reflect economic group interests. I also expect legislatures in initiative states to respond to interest group pressures by passing different laws than do legislatures in noninitiative states. Further analyses of the campaign finance data, plus comparisons of policies in the fifty states, provide strong empirical evidence that is consistent with these expectations.

Together, these theoretical and empirical results show that citizen and economic interest groups use direct legislation for different purposes and to different ends. The largely conservative and indirect influence by economic interest groups is a form of influence much different from—although perhaps no less important than—the one portrayed by modern critics of direct legislation.

Resources versus Preferences

Before discussing the motivation and justification of my study, it is instructive to compare my approach to a plausible alternative approach. Critics of my resource theory of interest group choice may argue that it is not a group's comparative advantage at mobilizing resources that determines which political strategies it chooses. Rather, these choices may result strictly from a group's preferences. Specifically, the argument goes, groups with more conservative policy preferences may find that political strategies aimed at preserving the status quo make the most sense. Change-oriented groups may, by contrast, find that policies modifying the status quo are better suited to achieving their goals. To the extent that economic interest groups are oriented more toward the status quo and citizen groups are oriented more toward change,[7] then one might observe precisely the patterns of direct legislation choice predicted by my resource theory and resulting strictly from differences in interest group preferences.

In fact, this preference-based argument has much merit. We would not be surprised to find groups that favor the status quo working to preserve policy and groups that oppose the status quo working to change it. The problem with

---

[7] This is a widely held but generally untested assumption.

this preference-based argument, however, is that it begs the question of where those preferences come from in the first place. Why are some groups, particularly economic interest groups, conservative? Why are others, particularly citizen groups, more change-oriented?

My approach provides a compelling answer to these questions. I argue that a group's preferences derive from its membership base and hence its resource advantages. Economic interest groups are able to mobilize particular types of resources that allow them to influence legislative policies but that may be used less effectively for changing policy through direct legislation. In other words, they are conservative precisely because they have been able to influence the status quo. Other groups such as citizen groups are able to mobilize different resources. Although these resources may be used to mobilize electoral support, they are less useful for influencing the legislative status quo. These citizen groups, then, are more change-oriented in the context of direct legislation precisely because they have been unable to influence policy through more traditional means.

There is also a second sense in which a group's preferences may relate to its choice of political strategies. Here the relevant point is the extremity of a group's position, relative to the preferences of the electorate. Extremity is important in the sense that it affects how difficult it is for a group to mobilize an electoral majority. Groups whose preferences and policy positions are close to the voting majority may be able to use their resources to mobilize an electoral majority much more easily than groups whose preferences and policy positions are extreme relative to those of most voters. In this case, a group's preferences affect the attractiveness of alternative political strategies by determining the amount of resources necessary to mobilize an electoral majority. Hence, what is important is not simply whether the group's preferences are moderate or extreme. Rather, a group's preferences, and their relation to those of the decisive voters, determine the effective costs of alternative political strategies.

Motivation: The Study of Interest Group Influence

In recent years, the highly visible increase in interest group involvement in politics has generated intense scholarly attention to the question of interest group influence. Indeed, many critics of the modern direct legislation process argue that the promise of direct legislation is compromised precisely by the ability of interest groups to manipulate direct legislation outcomes to their advantage. My research addresses the question of interest group influence in one political arena, the direct legislation process. As part of the larger literature on interest group influence, however, one of the main objectives of this research is to contribute to a broader understanding of interest group influence in politics.

I define an *interest group* as any organization that pursues its collective goals through the political process. This definition includes newly formed, transitory associations that organize for the sole purpose of achieving a single policy outcome as well as established, existing organizations with ongoing operations. The definition includes organizations with a very narrow focus as well as multi-issue, multipurpose organizations. It includes small organizations with only a few members as well as large organizations. However, it excludes individuals who autonomously attempt to affect policy and political parties whose primary goal is to promote candidates for elective office.[8]

I require an interest group to have some degree of formal organizational structure. At a minimum, members must recognize themselves as a group.[9] Among the groups I study empirically in later chapters, the degree of organizational structure ranges from very informal with loose rules and minimal structure to highly formalized with elaborate rules and procedures.

An interest group must also have a collective goal or goals. Indeed, people do not join a group unless they share with other members a belief in some unifying goal, even if this goal is merely to help them more easily attain individual benefits. I also focus on interest groups whose collective goal is political (i.e., the goal is attainable through use of the political process) and who choose strategies that involve the use of direct legislation.[10]

Regardless of whether they are primarily political or nonpolitical, formal or informal, single-purpose or multipurpose, all interest groups seek to promote their interests through the political process. Their ability to do so raises one of the fundamental questions in modern democratic government: How much power or autonomy should political interest groups have? Madison, for

[8] Individuals do not face the same sorts of collective action and coordination problems as organizations because their goals are, by definition, not collective. The definition does include individuals who act through a committee or organization. It also includes individual corporations.

[9] It is useful to differentiate an interest group, as defined here, from a latent group that is yet to form. Through its potential to organize and act, a latent group may be able to influence policy indirectly. To gain access to the mechanisms of political power and directly influence policy, however, it must be at least minimally organized.

[10] I tailor my definition of interest groups to the context of direct legislation. Therefore, it differs from extant definitions in studies of policy making in the U.S. Congress. My definition is narrower than most definitions because I focus on groups that use political strategies. It is broader than most because it includes transitory groups that mobilize for the purpose of using the political process to pursue an immediate public policy goal and because it includes nonvoluntary organizations, such as corporations, in addition to voluntary ones. Walker (1991), for example, considered only ongoing voluntary associations and their sources of financial support, whereas Salisbury (1984) also examined nonvoluntary organizations.

Note that the interest groups I study need not be strictly political. Many interest groups have nonpolitical activities that may be either primary or secondary to their political activities. Many groups or organizations, however, are strictly apolitical; these would not be included in my definition of interest groups. For example, many social or recreational clubs choose not to participate in politics, even through they have the organizational capacity to do so. Nonpolitical groups might, at some point, choose to pursue a political strategy, at which time they would become an interest group according to this definition.

example, argued that diverse (economic) interests "grow up of necessity in civilised nations" and that "(t)he regulation of these various and interfering interests forms the principal task of modern legislation" (James Madison in Hamilton et al., 1961, p. 79). In the modern political science literature, the (often implicit) debate concerning interest group influence is played out between those who believe that interest groups have a major influence in policy making and those who believe that their influence is more limited. This debate is rooted in two related literatures, the classic pluralist literature and the modern empirical literature on interest group influence in Congress.

The Pluralist Approach

According to the pluralist approach, interest groups are central actors in American politics (e.g., Truman 1951; Bentley 1967). Pluralists characterize the political system as a competition between interest groups. Groups are portrayed as sharing power across the political, economic, and social arenas (see Dahl 1961) and across policy domains (see Lowi 1969).[11]

By framing the political process as a competition between groups, the pluralist approach has profoundly affected the way political scientists view politics and political outcomes. Its conclusions about power sharing spawned a generation of critics, however. One critique of pluralism is that it does not address why some groups are more powerful than others (see Schattschneider 1960; McConnell 1966; Schlozman 1984; Schlozman and Tierney 1986). These critics argue that not all groups can overcome the barriers to effective representation. Revisionists such as Olson (1965), Salisbury (1969), Wilson (1974), and Walker (1991) showed that a group's ability to organize and participate in the political process depends on its internal characteristics. From this perspective, groups vary in the resources available to them, and these resources in turn determine their effectiveness.

The Congressional Approach

Whereas the classic pluralist and revisionist literatures provide a theoretical foundation for understanding interest group influence, the recent literature on interest group influence in Congress provides an empirical foundation. In his

---

[11] Lowi argued that particular groups focus on influencing only certain policy domains. For example, he argued that agricultural policy is dominated by agricultural interest groups, regulatory policy by interest groups in the regulated industry, etc. Although Lowi's theory is consistent with the pluralists in that both observe a multiplicity of interests, it is in conflict with the pluralists in emphasizing a lack of competition between groups in a given policy area.

comprehensive review of this literature, Smith (1995) described a body of research that is sophisticated, diverse, and growing. Nearly two hundred books and scholarly papers published in the last decade address the role and influence of interest groups in Congress.

Much of the recent literature focuses on the effects of interest group campaign contributions and lobbying activities.[12] Although contemporary scholars agree that interest group activities have changed in quality and quantity over the last several decades, they debate the policy consequences of these changes. As Smith noted, some studies find evidence of statistically significant relationships between campaign contributions and legislative voting behavior and between lobbying and voting behavior.[13] Other studies find little or no such evidence.[14] In fact, the distinctive feature of the recent literature on interest group influence in Congress is that the results are so decidedly mixed.[15]

My Approach

My approach to studying interest group influence allows me to examine simultaneously the major issues raised in each literature. As do the pluralist and revisionist literatures, I recognize the multiplicity of interest groups and compare the relative power of several different types of groups (economic vs. citizen, wealthy vs. less wealthy, narrow vs. broad-based). As does the revisionist literature, I recognize that the very existence of such diverse groups is a function of their internal characteristics and their ability to overcome inherent hurdles. And, as does the congressional literature, I examine interest group influence directly.

My approach combines some of the most important contributions of the pluralist, revisionist, and congressional literatures. Whereas the pluralists focus strictly on the ability of groups to organize or engage in political action,

[12] For similar research at the state level, see Gray and Lowery (1996) and Thomas and Hrebenar (1996).

[13] On the relationship between contributions and voting behavior, Smith cited Silberman and Durden (1976), Welch (1982), Feldstein and Melnick (1984), Peltzman (1984), Coughlin (1985), Ashford (1986), Ginsberg and Green (1986), Jones and Keiser (1987), Saltzman (1987), Wilhite and Theilmann (1987), Masters and Zardkoohi (1988), McArthur and Marks (1988), Langbein and Lotwis (1990), Durden et al. (1991), Stratmann (1991), and Fleisher (1993). On the relationship between lobbying and voting behavior, Smith cited Smith (1984, 1993), Wright (1990), Rothenberg (1992), and Segal et al. (1992).

[14] See Chappell (1981, 1982), Wright (1985), Kabashima and Sato (1986), Owens (1986), Grenzke (1989a, b), Vesenka (1989), and Rothenberg (1992) on campaign contributions. See Kalt and Zupan (1984), Fowler and Shaiko (1987), Langbein and Lotwis (1990) on lobbying.

[15] Smith offered four possible reasons for this ambiguity: methodological problems; complex interest group motivations; conditional effects that depend on variation in issues, policies, and especially electoral circumstances; and indirect effects (i.e., influence over aspects of behavior other than roll call votes).

I consider how their internal characteristics affect the strategies groups choose. And whereas the congressional scholars examine interest group influence explicitly, I extend the scope of these analyses to compare the influence of different types of groups in different political settings. By combining the most promising contributions of each literature, my approach provides a detailed but intuitive statement about the relationship among a group's internal characteristics, activities, and influence.

This is not to say that my work is the first to link interest group characteristics and environmental factors with an analysis of the choices groups make. In his important new book, Kollman (1998) established—both theoretically and empirically—important differences in interest groups' decisions to use outside (i.e., grassroots mobilizing) lobbying strategies. In contrast to my approach, however, Kollman focused on external factors related to an issue—such as the stage of legislation and the underlying salience of the issue—as the primary factors affecting a group's decision to engage in grassroots mobilization. My approach, by contrast, considers how both a group's internal characteristics and resources *and* the institutional and behavioral hurdles associated with each strategy *interact* to affect a group's decisions. Walker (1991) similarly focused on a group's resources, specifically on the sources of its support, as constraints on a group's activities. And Berry (1977) posited a "decision-making framework" in which a group's organizational capacities combine with the external opportunities it faces to affect its choice of issues, strategies, and tactics. I see my work as building on the theoretical and empirical insights generated by these approaches.

My approach also provides a context for making sense of the apparently contradictory results in the empirical literature on interest group influence in Congress. According to the logic of my theory, groups try to adopt strategies that maximize their influence, while considering the benefits and costs of pursuing those strategies. Some groups are more successful than others at finding appropriate strategies. When a group selects a strategy that requires the resources it has or is able to amass, it may succeed in influencing policy. Most studies of interest group influence in Congress focus on a small set of strategies, specifically making campaign contributions and direct lobbying. Some groups will have the necessary resources to achieve influence through the use of these strategies, whereas others will not. Thus, a compelling and theoretically grounded explanation for the contradictory results on interest group influence is that some studies consider groups that are well suited for the strategies they analyze, whereas other studies consider groups that lack the resources to influence policy in these ways. This view, by extension, raises the possibility that groups that appear less influential in the existing studies may simply be pursuing forms of influence other than those traditionally analyzed by interest group scholars.

Justification: Why Study Direct Legislation?

Though the theory developed in this book deals with the general question of interest group influence, the specific application is to group influence in the direct legislation process. Direct legislation is policy making at the ballot box. The four types of direct legislation include direct initiatives, indirect initiatives, popular referendums, and submitted referendums.[16] In the *direct initiative*, an interest group drafts a proposition and qualifies it for the ballot by collecting a prespecified number of voter signatures. If the measure qualifies, it is placed on the ballot and citizens vote on it. In the *indirect initiative*, a group drafts and qualifies a proposition, then submits it to the legislature for consideration. If the legislature passes the measure, then it becomes law. Otherwise, the measure is placed on the ballot, and voters decide its fate. In the *popular referendum*, the legislature passes a law according to its regular procedures, and a group subsequently petitions to have the measure placed on the ballot for ratification or rejection by the electorate. In the *submitted referendum*, the legislature passes a law and places it on the ballot without the formal intervention of an interest group.

In all four types of direct legislation, propositions can be either statutory or constitutional. *Statutory* propositions change existing statutes, whereas *constitutional* propositions change provisions of the state constitution. Initiatives and referendums can be *binding*, taking the force of law upon passage, or *advisory*, requiring further legislative action before they become laws.

Of the four types of direct legislation, the direct initiative has drawn the most attention. The direct initiative is the purest form of direct democracy in the sense that citizens and interest groups are solely responsible for making policy without the intervention of elected representatives. Thus, the direct initiative contains the greatest potential for interest group influence. Many of the most widely publicized and exorbitantly financed direct legislation propositions are initiatives.[17] Still, groups may use the other three forms of direct legislation to influence policy, so I include those types in my study as well.

[16] Although the recall was an important component of the Progressive-era reform packages in many states, it differs from the four forms of direct legislation in a critically important way: citizens vote for or against elected representatives rather than for or against policy directly. I do not focus on recall elections in this research.

[17] Some of the most expensive initiatives in my sample include Proposal C (Michigan 1992), a property tax/school funding initiative in which supporters and opponents spent over $3 million; Measure 5 (Oregon 1992), an initiative proposal to close temporarily the Trojan nuclear facility in which nearly $5 million was spent; Proposition 99 (California 1988), a cigarette and tobacco tax initiative in which over $21 million was spent; Proposition 128 (California 1990), an environmental measure in which nearly $22 million was spent; and Proposition 134 (California 1990), an alcohol surtax, in which over $41 million was spent.

Nearly all democracies use some form of direct legislation. The democracies of Western Europe, Canada, Australia, New Zealand, and now Eastern Europe have used national referendums to register popular support for major issues such as the adoption of a new constitution or major constitutional revisions. Referendums are also used to address territorial and jurisdictional issues such as secession from a colonial empire, dissolution of a republic into smaller states, and membership in an international organization such as the United Nations or the European Community (see Butler and Ranney 1994). They are used to decide moral issues such as abortion, divorce, or prohibition; political issues such as changes in the voting age; and other issues such as changes in daylight saving time (see Butler and Ranney 1994). Switzerland is perhaps the most famous user of direct legislation, using initiatives and referendums to decide a wide range of public policy issues. In fact, Progressive reformers in the United States looked to Switzerland as a model for designing direct legislation institutions in the American states.[18]

The United States, by contrast, offers no national initiative or referendum, but direct legislation is used extensively at the state and local levels. Currently, twenty states allow binding direct initiatives at the statewide level.[19] Ten states allow indirect initiatives;[20] twenty-one states allow popular referendums; and nearly all allow submitted referendums (Dubois and Feeney 1992). Appendix A reports provisions for the use of statewide direct legislation in the United States.

Although a total of twenty-six states allow some form of direct legislation, the frequency with which it is used varies a great deal from state to state. In some states, direct legislation is a central component of the political landscape. In California, Oregon, and North Dakota, for example, nearly every ballot contains multiple propositions covering a wide range of issues. In these states, the laws resulting from direct legislation often have important policy consequences. Recent propositions have changed policy in areas such as taxation, education, welfare, public health and safety, electoral laws, immigration, gay rights, access to abortion, criminal laws, and civil laws. In other states, by contrast, direct legislation is rarely used. Two states (Illinois and Wyoming) had no initiatives on the statewide ballot from 1981 to 1990, and

---

[18] In recent years, the Italians have also used direct legislation with greater frequency. The Italian constitution now allows groups to call a referendum on any prior legislation, not just recently passed laws, effectively allowing any measure to be put before voters as in the initiative.

[19] Michigan, Ohio, and Nevada allow direct initiatives for constitutional amendments but indirect initiatives only for statutes. Utah and Washington allow direct and indirect initiatives for statutory measures.

[20] Alaska, Maine, Massachusetts, Mississippi, and Wyoming allow only indirect initiatives, with Alaska and Wyoming allowing the legislature the option of whether to consider the measure, and Utah and Washington allowing indirect statutory initiatives as the sponsor's option. Michigan, Ohio, and Nevada allow indirect initiatives only for statutory measures. Mississippi allows indirect initiatives only for constitutional amendments.

five others had five initiatives or fewer (Public Affairs Research Institute of New Jersey 1992).

Regardless of whether or not one lives in or studies a state or country that uses direct legislation, the direct legislation process provides a unique laboratory for understanding more general aspects of politics. One of the most interesting of these aspects is the role of interest groups in political campaigns. Avenues for interest group influence in direct legislation are plentiful and transparent, making direct legislation elections an ideal case study. To see why, consider the following facts about direct legislation.

First, voters in direct legislation elections choose policy directly rather than electing representatives who choose policy on their behalf. As a result, direct legislation, especially the initiative, lacks the deliberative quality of legislative policy making. Although legislative deliberation may generate problems of its own, *no* such formal deliberative medium, however imperfect, exists in the initiative process. Even though representatives may "refine" policy in the early stages of the referendum process, voters still have ultimate decision-making authority.[21] Therefore, to the extent that interest groups are able to manipulate or mislead voters, the lack of deliberation means that an important external check on groups' influence is absent.

Second, many direct legislation propositions are complex, technical, and unfamiliar to voters. Voters therefore tend to have very little prior information about, or understanding of, the propositions they are asked to evaluate. Few actors besides organized interest groups themselves are likely to have such substantive information. As a result, voters who desire information about the content of propositions have few alternatives but to rely on interest groups for that information. When interest groups can influence the channels of political communication, they may be able to use their informational advantages to mislead voters.[22]

Third, many of the short cuts and low information cues that voters rely on when they lack information in candidate elections are absent in direct legislation elections. Perhaps the most important cue that is missing is partisanship. In candidate elections, voters can infer a great deal about a candidate's policy positions and likely voting behavior simply by learning his or her partisanship. In such cases, it may be both convenient and rational to vote on the basis of party. In direct legislation elections, by contrast, partisan cues are generally absent. Although partisan candidates and officials may endorse particular initiatives and referendums, political parties rarely do. Therefore, party cues—so important to voters in other settings—are absent or ambiguous in direct

---

[21] Although voter decisions in direct legislation are unmediated by other government actors, they are still subject to judicial review.

[22] Lupia (1997) and Lupia and McCubbins (1998) explored both the opportunities for, and limitations of, such deceptions.

legislation campaigns. Candidates also have past histories from which voters may learn about a candidate's likely future actions. New policy initiatives have no such history, making the voters' problems all the more complicated. The absence of useful cues makes direct legislation voters especially reliant on substantive information disseminated by interest groups during the campaign.[23]

The preceding facts suggest that the opportunities for interest group influence are plentiful, and additional facts show that these opportunities are transparent as well. For example, when a representative legislature makes policy, interest groups have no power to change laws directly. Instead, they must persuade legislators to pass favorable policies. These legislators also face pressures from other interest groups, other legislators, constituents, and party leaders. Because the interaction of such pressures with the legislator's own preferences determine his or her actions (Kingdon 1989), isolating the independent effect of any one actor on a legislator's decisions is extremely difficult. In the direct legislation process, by contrast, voters who ultimately decide policy are typically targeted only by interest groups. Hence, voters face fewer formal pressures than do legislators. As a result, isolating the effects of interest group activities on voter choice may be easier than isolating the equivalent effect on legislators because there are relatively few mediating factors in direct legislation.

Also helpful in measuring interest group influence is the fact that the relationship between interest groups and voters is more limited than the relationship between interest groups and legislators. In the legislative process, interest groups and legislators engage in ongoing exchange relationships. Interest groups offer campaign contributions in an attempt to secure favorable policy, and legislators may give service and policy for financial contributions and other forms of support. Conversely, in the direct legislation process, voters depend on interest groups for information, but they need not rely on them for future benefits. The relationship is thus more limited and more closely tied to the immediate task of voting on a single proposition. Indeed, many of the interest groups involved in direct legislation form for the purpose of supporting or opposing a single proposition and disband soon after the voting occurs. It may therefore be easier to assess the policy consequences of an interest group's actions in the case of direct legislation.

Despite these important reasons for studying direct legislation and the influence of interest groups in the process, the subject has received scant scholarly attention, primarily because of a lack of readily available and reliable data.

---

[23] Voters in direct legislation elections may use other cues not available in candidate elections. Research by Lupia (1994) showed that voters who know the interests of groups involved in direct legislation campaigns can use this information to infer how to vote. For example, Lupia found that voters who were able to identify which of the five insurance initiatives on the 1988 California ballot were endorsed by the insurance industry were more likely to cast votes that were in their economic self-interest.

Data from some states are incomplete or unavailable. Fortunately, several other states rival or surpass most national governments in terms of the quality and quantity of political and election data they produce, and I rely heavily on these in my research. Even when data are available from some or all states, however, they are rarely compiled in a convenient form and made easily accessible. Despite this shortcoming, I assert that the advantages of studying state-level political processes outweigh the problems of data availability. States exhibit a great deal of institutional variation that simply does not exist at the national level. As Erikson et. al (1993) argued, states provide an excellent laboratory for comparative analyses of institutional processes. I follow in that tradition, using the analysis of state-level direct legislation processes to draw general conclusions about what allows certain interest groups to influence policy. Even though the primary focus of this book is the state-level direct legislation process, the theoretical framework and many of my conclusions apply to questions about policy-making processes at other levels of government.

Plan of the Book

In this chapter, I presented the intuition behind, and conclusions derived from, my theory of interest group influence. In the next three chapters, I more thoroughly develop the major components of my theoretical framework. Each chapter corresponds to one or more of the theory's five basic premises. In chapter 2, I describe the forms of influence that interest groups can hope to achieve. I develop my analogy to the profit-maximizing firm and the logic of interest group choice. I then present a simple model to identify the conditions under which groups can achieve each form of influence. In chapter 3, I describe the hurdles to achieving direct and indirect forms of influence that direct legislation creates. In chapter 4, I describe a correspondence between interest groups' bases of support, their comparative advantages at mobilizing monetary and personnel resources, and their ability to pursue direct and indirect forms of influence. I then generate a set of empirically testable hypotheses about the direct legislation strategies that interest groups with different internal characteristics will choose.

In chapters 5 through 7, I test these hypotheses and their implications for interest group influence. In chapter 5, I analyze data from several sources to test hypotheses about the activities groups pursue and their motivations for using direct legislation. The first data source is a survey that asks interest groups about their political activities and motivations. I use the survey data to test hypotheses about the forms of influence that groups pursue and the activities they undertake. The second data source consists of campaign finance records from direct legislation contributors in several states. The campaign finance records show the patterns of contribution activities by various types of groups. I use the campaign finance data to test hypotheses about how interest groups allocate their financial resources and hence about how they pursue influence.

In chapter 6, I further analyze the campaign finance data to assess the aggregate consequences of interest group choice on policy outcomes. I show that ballot measure campaign contributions from citizen groups are associated with higher passage rates, whereas contributions from economic groups translate into lower passage rates. I also show that economic and citizen groups contribute to ballot measures in different subject areas, and that the ballot measures that ultimately pass reflect these substantive differences. Together, these analyses show that direct legislation outcomes reflect the ability of citizen groups to pursue direct modifying influence and the ability of economic groups to pursue direct preserving influence.

In chapter 7, I test hypotheses about indirect influence. I first compare policy outcomes in initiative and noninitiative states and find important and significant differences in some policy areas. I then conduct detailed multivariate analyses of two policies—parental consent for teenage abortions and the death penalty—to isolate the effect of interest group pressures on state legislative policy. Together, chapters 6 and 7 provide the empirical basis for assessing the conditions under which interest groups can use the direct legislation process to affect policy.

In chapter 8, I evaluate the populist paradox in light of my theoretical and empirical evidence. I conclude that, although the populist paradox takes a form different from the one alleged by modern critics of direct legislation, it is, nevertheless, a paradox. Wealthy economic interest groups are severely constrained by the institutional and behavioral hurdles inherent in the direct legislation process. They cannot and do not use their financial resources to "buy" legislation that is detrimental to broader citizen interests. Direct legislation does, however, provide economic interest groups with an important additional means for protecting the status quo and influencing state legislators. This influence may be every bit as important as passing new laws by initiative, especially for groups that already have substantial influence in the legislative process. Thus, although economic interests can use direct legislation to influence policy, the forms of influence they can achieve are quite different than direct legislation's critics charge.

2

Interest Group Choice

THE FIRST TWO PREMISES in my theory of interest group influence describe what influence groups can hope to achieve. In this chapter, I first discuss the forms of influence available through the direct legislation process. I then present my theory in more formal terms and use it to illustrate when groups can achieve each form of influence.

Forms of Influence

Groups can promote their political interests by pursuing one or more forms of influence. I argue that influence can modify or preserve the status quo; it can also be direct or indirect. *Modifying* influence involves changing policy by passing a new law. *Preserving* influence involves protecting the status quo by preventing the passage of new laws. *Direct* influence involves undertaking activities in one policy arena to affect policy in that same arena (i.e., putting an initiative on the ballot for the immediate purpose of implementing a particular policy). *Indirect* influence involves using one policy-making mechanism (i.e., the initiative process) to bring about an effect on policy in another policy-making arena (i.e., the legislative process). Modifying influence can be either direct or indirect, as can preserving influence. Therefore, the four types of influence are: direct modifying, direct preserving, indirect modifying, and indirect preserving. Table 2.1 provides examples of each form of influence.

Understanding Direct Influence

Direct influence involves affecting policy through a given policy-making mechanism. An example of *direct modifying influence* involves passing a new law by initiative. This influence is modifying in the sense that the policy consequence is to replace the status quo with a new law. It is direct in the sense that the change comes about as a consequence of the initiative rather than from legislators responding to interest groups' use of direct legislation.

Direct modifying influence occurs whenever a ballot measure passes. In the 1996 general election, statewide initiatives and referendums passed in such diverse subject areas as campaign finance reform, the environment, gambling,

TABLE 2.1
Forms of Influence

Form of Influence	Direct	Indirect
Modifying	Pass direct initiative or submitted referendum	Pass indirect initiative Support initiative or submitted referendum
Preserving	Block initiative or submitted referendum Pass popular referendum	Oppose initiative or submitted referendum

taxation, and term limits. In each case, groups that expended resources to promote the measures were successful in achieving direct modifying influence. This is not to say, of course, that any one group's efforts were decisive or that the measures would have failed in the absence of a given group's efforts. Rather, the point is that, in coalition with other supporting groups, the direct legislation strategies these groups undertook were associated with the passage of a new initiative.

To achieve direct modifying influence, groups must amass an electoral majority in support of a proposed initiative. On some issues—for example, when a large bloc of voters is predisposed toward favoring the measure—mobilizing an electoral majority may be easy. On other issues—for example, when voters have yet to form an opinion or when a large bloc of voters is predisposed toward opposing the measure—mobilizing an electoral majority may be difficult.

An example of *direct preserving influence* involves blocking the passage of an initiative. Such influence is preserving in the sense that it prevents a change to the status quo; it is direct in the sense that the effect is made through the initiative process. A second example of direct preserving influence involves passing a popular referendum to repeal a law recently passed by the legislature. Such influence is preserving in the sense that its consequence is to return policy to the previous status quo (i.e., the one that existed before the legislature passed its law). It is direct in the sense that the effect is an immediate consequence of the referendum.[1]

Direct preserving influence occurs whenever a ballot measure fails. In the 1996 general election, initiatives and referendums failed in the areas of healthcare reform, insurance reform, and term limits. Groups that expended resources to defeat the measures were successful in achieving direct preserving

[1] Although the use of popular referendums typically involves returning policy to the preexisting status quo, the use of submitted referendums involves passing a new law, that is, changing policy from the status quo to a new policy.

influence. Again, the point is not that any one group's efforts were decisive in defeating the measures nor that the measures would have passed in the absence of a given interest group's activities. The point is that, in coalition with other opposing groups, these groups undertook direct legislation strategies associated with the defeat of the initiatives and referendums they opposed.

To achieve direct preserving influence, groups must amass an electoral majority. Unlike groups whose objective is to modify the status quo, however, these groups must amass a majority *against* the measure. As I will show in chapter 3, the way voters make decisions in direct legislation elections and the way they treat risk means that for some groups, mobilizing a majority against a measure may be easier than mobilizing a majority in support.

Most existing studies of interest group influence focus on direct forms of influence, particularly direct modifying influence. For instance, most of the literature on interest group influence in Congress examines the ability of groups to use campaign contributions and/or lobbying strategies to exert direct influence over legislator behavior (for a comprehensive review, see Smith 1995). The few existing studies of interest group influence in the initiative process also focus on direct influence. For example, Lowenstein (1982) and Owens and Wade (1986) study the extent to which financial contributions to ballot measure campaign committees translate into a measure's failure or success. As such, direct influence has received the most attention in the existing literature.

Understanding Indirect Influence

Indirect influence comes about when an actor uses one policy arena to pressure actors in another policy arena to change or protect policy. An example of *indirect modifying influence* involves using initiatives to pressure state legislators to pass a new law.[2] An example of *indirect preserving influence* involves using initiatives to pressure state legislators to block passage of new legislation. There are at least two ways an interest group can use initiatives to pressure state legislators. The first is to threaten to propose and pass an initiative that legislators oppose. The second is to use initiatives to signal the group's support for or against an issue. Each of these approaches involves pursuing different strategies, and each entails different relationships among interest groups, voters, and legislators.

To pressure legislators by proposing or threatening to propose an adverse initiative, interest groups must be able to make a credible threat to pass the initiative directly. Otherwise, legislators can simply ignore the interest group's

[2] In this research, I focus on the use of initiatives to pressure legislators in an interest group's state. Interest groups may also use initiatives to pressure other policy actors such as bureaucrats, legislators in other states, and members of Congress.

threat.[3] Several conditions must be met for the interest group's threat to be credible. First, the group must be able to amass the necessary resources to sponsor an initiative. Second, the group and a majority of voters must be sufficiently aligned to be able to overturn the status quo. Both of these conditions depend, to a large extent, on the relationship among interest group, voter, and legislator preferences. I consider this relationship and its consequences for interest group influence later in this chapter.

One example in which interest groups clearly took steps to pressure state legislators, and the legislature responded by passing favorable legislation, occurred in the area of environmental regulation in California.[4] Before 1993, numerous efforts to reform the environmental protection regulations contained in the California Environmental Quality Act (CEQA) had failed in the California state legislature. In response, a number of organizations formed a coalition called CART (Citizens Against Red Tape) to lobby in favor of reforming the CEQA. Several subsequent reforms were introduced in the legislature. Although the opponents of these reforms argued that they were too favorable to the California Chamber of Commerce and the petroleum industry, both well represented in CART, the measures ultimately passed. Whether their passage directly resulted from CART's effort is impossible to know for certain. However, Barber (1993, p. 37) noted that there was "fear that CART might try to change the law through the initiative route if it did not get its way in the Legislature. As evidence of this fear, environmentalists pointed to CART's hiring of Woodward-McDowell—a public relations company specializing in ballot measure campaigns."

A second and even more dramatic example of legislators responding to an interest group's initiative threat occurred recently in the area of charter school regulation in California. For many years, charter school proponents have tried unsuccessfully to persuade the state legislature to liberalize its restrictions regarding the establishment of and control over charter schools. In the spring of 1998, proponents of charter school reform established a committee called the Technology Network and began circulating petitions to qualify an initiative for the November 1998 ballot. From the beginning, the proponents made it clear that they would withdraw the petitions if the legislature itself passed acceptable legislation. In May 1998, the legislature and governor did just that, passing AB 544, which (among other things) authorized additional charter schools and made it easier for parents to start charter schools. As promised, proponents withdrew their petitions.

The second way interest groups can use initiatives to pressure the state legislature is to use initiatives to signal the groups' support for or opposition to an issue. To signal their position, groups can expend money or other scarce re-

[3] For legislators to respond to an interest group's threat, they must have preferences over policy outcomes. These preferences may come about because of personal preferences or responsiveness to constituencies.

[4] Much of this discussion draws from Barber (1993).

sources. By observing that a group chose to expend resources to support or oppose a measure, legislators can infer that the group expects to gain from the outcome of the election. Otherwise, the group would use its resources for some other purposes. In these circumstances, interest group expenditures (whether in terms of money, volunteer support, or other resources) serve as a costly, and therefore credible, signal to the legislature of the intensity of the interest group's preferences.[5]

Under what conditions do we expect interest groups to be able to use initiatives to signal their preferences through direct legislation? For the legislature to respond to an interest group's pressure, three conditions must be met. The first condition is that the group has sufficient resources to attract the legislature's attention. Some groups feel strongly about an issue but lack the resources to organize and finance an initiative campaign. Groups that lack resources may be unable to engage in campaign activities that would attract the legislature's attention.

The second necessary condition is that the group must have something legislators want. In particular, in exchange for legislators' attention, groups must be able to promise either future campaign contributions or the backing of a large, important electoral constituency. If the group lacks these resources, it cannot promise future payment for the legislators' cooperation. Therefore, even if the group successfully signals its position, legislators have little incentive to respond to the group's signal.

The third necessary condition is that legislators must be electorally vulnerable. When legislators face tough competition and their jobs are at risk, they have a greater incentive to respond to the demands of important constituencies. When they are electorally secure, legislators can instead focus on other goals besides re-election (Fenno 1978).[6]

Note that a ballot measure need not pass for it to provide an effective signal of an interest group's preferences. Indeed, to achieve indirect influence, the signal rather than the outcome is key. When groups expend resources to signal their position, what matters are the interest group's behavior, the costs it is willing to incur to support or oppose the measure, and perhaps the response of important electoral constituencies.[7]

The two approaches to indirect influence differ in important ways. In the first approach, legislators and interest groups have divergent policy prefer-

---

[5] For a review of the literature on costly action in signaling games in political science, see Lupia (1992).

[6] Many observers argue that there are now few safe seats in state legislatures. As the number of states enacting term limits increases, seats are likely to become even less secure, and the insulating effect of incumbency is likely to be much less important. These recent changes in state political environments are likely to result in more competitive elections and seats. Consequently, state legislators have more incentive to pay attention to the issue preferences of their electoral constituencies.

[7] The legislature may respond to support by a constituency that makes up far less than an electoral majority (see Fenno 1978).

ences. The interest group's strategy is therefore to establish that it can and will propose an initiative in response to the legislature's action or inaction. If the group can mobilize the necessary resources, and if there is sufficient voter support, then the legislature responds to avert the initiative proposal. By contrast, in the second approach, legislators and interest groups agree on policy. Therefore, the interest group's strategy is not to establish that it has the resources to punish the legislature with an adverse initiative. Instead, the interest group uses the initiative to signal its position to the legislature. Another difference between the two approaches to indirect influence is that once the legislature obtains information about the group's preferences, it uses this information for different purposes. In the first form of indirect influence, the legislature uses information about the group's preferences to avert initiative proposals. In the second form, the legislature learns about the group's preferences from its initiative proposal and campaign activities and uses this information as it formulates future legislative proposals.

Recent California politics provides examples of groups expending resources in initiative campaigns to signal their positions to the legislature. One example occurred in the area of health industry regulation. In 1996, labor organizations placed two initiatives, Propositions 214 and 216, on the California ballot. Nearly identical in content, these two propositions would have regulated many of the operations of health maintenance organizations (HMOs) in the state. Proposition 214 was proposed, supported, and largely funded by the Service Employees International Union and AFL-CIO. Proposition 216 was proposed, supported, and largely funded by the California Nurses Association. After a grueling campaign period and expensive campaigns both for and against the initiatives, both initiatives failed. In the three months immediately following the 1996 general election, however, the state legislature proposed at least twenty-seven HMO regulation bills that included many of the provisions contained in the initiative measures.[8] Although none of these bills have passed both houses of the state legislature at the time of this writing, twenty-three are still under consideration. By contrast, only one HMO regulation bill was introduced during the entire twelve-month period before the 1996 election. Thus, while the HMO regulation bills introduced in early 1997 may or may not have been introduced as a direct consequence of the failed initiatives, the increase in the number of bills in this area since their failure seems far too great to be considered coincidental.

Parallels to Influence in the Legislative Arena

These forms of influence have important analogues in other policy-making arenas. First, along the modifying-preserving dimension, interest groups' lob-

---

[8] California Bill Tracking Statenet (1997).

bying and contributing activities may be aimed at pressuring the legislature either to modify or to preserve the status quo. Many of the works on interest group influence surveyed by Smith (1995) tend to focus on groups' ability to modify the status quo. This emphasis in the empirical literature is no doubt driven by both normative and practical concerns. Normatively, the ability of interest groups to change policy through spending and lobbying activities may raise greater concerns than does their ability to block policy. Practically, empirical measures of modifying influence (i.e., Did the policy change?) may be easier to link to specific interest group activities than empirical measures of preserving influence (i.e., Did the policy remain?). Other more theoretical or conceptual works, however, have emphasized the gatekeeping powers of Congress (see especially Shepsle and Weingast 1987) and the ability of interest groups to preserve the status quo by pressuring members of Congress to keep adverse legislation off the congressional agenda.

Second, along the direct–indirect dimension, groups can adopt political strategies that produce either direct or indirect influence. Directly, groups can contribute to or lobby policymakers to persuade them to take particular policy positions. Indirectly, groups can influence other actors (i.e., voters, other interest groups, other policymakers) who in turn place pressure on legislators.

Interest group scholars have studied both direct and indirect forms of influence. Most empirical studies of interest group influence in Congress tend to focus on groups' ability to directly affect policymakers' decisions through their lobbying and contributions. Recent work by Walker (1991) and Kollman (1998) emphasized the use of outside lobbying strategies to influence legislative policymakers indirectly by mobilizing important grassroots constituencies. Together, these literatures find important evidence of both types of influence.

Interest Group Choice

How do groups choose which of the four forms of influence to pursue? I posit that groups make a cost-benefit calculation when they consider the forms of influence and political strategies available to them. Groups first assess their current resource base and calculate the cost of amassing additional resources. They next estimate the expected costs and benefits associated with each form of influence. This cost-benefit calculation allows groups to identify which forms of influence are available to them. From the set of feasible forms of influence, groups then choose a form of influence and a specific strategy for achieving the form of influence that maximizes their expected net benefit.

Some strategies can lead to numerous forms of influence. Thus, a group may undertake a given strategy with multiple goals in mind. For example, a group may contribute financial resources to an initiative campaign with the hope of helping to pass a new law. If the law does not pass, the group may still receive some benefits from its contribution if it provides pressure on state legislators to pass the same law themselves. Although the group may not have intended to exert this latter form of influence when it undertook its direct legislation strategy, the group may nonetheless benefit from such influence.

In the discussion of interest group choice below, I first elaborate my notion of group decision making as analogous to the profit-maximizing firm. I then present a simple model to identify the relationship among a group's resources, preferences, and influence.

Interest Groups and Firms

In many ways, my view of interest group behavior parallels the common view of the profit-maximizing firm in microeconomics. Firms choose between alternative modes of production. Each mode of production requires specific combinations of inputs; each promises some level of output. Firms seek the mode of production that is expected to generate the highest returns, net of the firm's costs, subject to internal (resource) constraints and external (technological and market-based) hurdles. Likewise, interest groups choose among many alternative political strategies. Groups anticipate some returns from each strategy and expect to pay some costs. Their ability to pay those costs depends on the group's ability to acquire and mobilize particular resources. Groups seek the political strategy that generates the highest expected net benefit, subject to various internal constraints and external hurdles. As with firms, the most important internal constraints an interest group faces are resource constraints. The most important external hurdles are the institutional and behavioral hurdles associated with each political strategy.

The profit-maximizing firm analogy is useful because it emphasizes the constrained maximization problem that both interest groups and profit-maximizing firms confront. Interest groups attempt to achieve their political influence by choosing among alternative political strategies. Firms attempt to earn profits by choosing among alternative modes of production. Both interest groups and firms evaluate the expected costs and benefits of alternative courses of action and choose those that promise the greatest net benefits. As with firms, uncertainty and limited resources restrict a group's ability to identify and pursue its optimal political strategy. A group's actual choices, like a firm's, may consequently diverge from the choices that a strict profit-maximizer would make.

Interest groups and firms share other common problems as well. Perhaps most important, the resources they can devote to a given production process or political strategy derive from the organization's internal characteristics. For example, firms can mobilize two types of resources, capital and labor. Similarly, interest groups can mobilize monetary resources, which, like capital, consist of cash and other financial assets, and personnel resources, which, like labor, consist of manpower and other forms of human capital. A given interest group's ability to raise and mobilize monetary and personnel resources depends on its membership characteristics. Some groups have membership bases that enable them to raise monetary resources at low cost; others must incur much higher costs to raise the same level of monetary resources and may instead find it more economical to raise personnel resources. A firm's ability to mobilize capital and labor also depends on its internal organizational characteristics as well as its market position and other external factors. For some firms, raising additional capital is relatively easy; for others, it is more difficult.

Focusing on choice—whether by firms or interest groups—makes the notion of trade-offs explicit. Firms select one or a few modes of production. In doing so, they forgo the benefits associated with other modes of production. They expend resources to obtain a given set of benefits rather than keep those resources or use them for some other purpose. Their choices mean that some new opportunities will become available and others will not. Interest groups also select one or more activities at the expense of others. The choice of one political strategy means that one set of benefits and opportunities is available to the group and other benefits and opportunities are sacrificed.

As with any analogy, there are limits to the parallels between interest groups and profit-maximizing firms. First, most of the external hurdles that interest groups face, particularly those resulting from institutional hurdles such as electoral laws, are fixed or at least are determined exogenously. In the language of economics, interest groups are "price takers." By contrast, firms are often able to affect prices by their actions; that is, they may be either price takers or price setters.[9]

The second limit to the analogy of the profit-maximizing firm results from the nature of an interest group's constituency. Most interest groups are voluntary associations that concern themselves, first and foremost, with membership recruitment and retention. Thus, their choice of political strategies is based not only on each strategy's expected policy consequence but also on each strategy's impact on the group's membership. Although firms may have some interest in promoting worker morale and social causes, they need not attribute the same importance to these concerns.

These limitations aside, however, the same basic logic of how firms choose among alternative modes of production underlies my conceptualization of how interest groups choose among alternative political strategies.

---

[9] In fact, under some circumstances, interest groups act as price setters, such as when interest group activities lead policy makers to change political institutions, when their behavior triggers responses by other actors that make it more or less difficult to overcome hurdles, or when they pursue measures that change the institutional rules. Such circumstances are secondary, however, to interest groups' more common problem of overcoming hurdles over which they have little or no control.

The logic of interest group choice embodied in this analogy provides the groundwork for generating hypotheses about the forms of influence groups will pursue, the strategies they will adopt, and the influence they will ultimately have. In the next section, I present a simple model of interest group choice that aids in understanding the determinants of interest group influence.

Achieving Influence

To illustrate how groups choose which forms of influence to pursue, I present a simple spatial model of interest group influence. The model shows how the resources a group must expend to achieve different forms of influence are related to the underlying preferences of the interest group, voters, and perhaps state legislators. The model allows me to show that under some preference configurations, the resources required to achieve direct modifying influence are relatively low. Under other configurations, even groups with vast resources will be unable to mobilize an electoral majority in support of an initiative and may be limited to direct preserving or indirect forms of influence. Extending the model, I also show the conditions under which groups will be able to achieve indirect influence through the direct legislation process.

The model represents a highly stylized view of the complex and often very messy policy process. Like all simple spatial models, it does not incorporate all features of the political landscape, but rather isolates aspects of the process that determine policy outcomes.

Achieving Direct Influence

I first illustrate the conditions under which groups can achieve direct influence. Consider the unidimensional policy space [0,1] as illustrated in figure 2.1. There are two players, an Interest Group and a Voter.[10] The object of the game is to select one of two policies, the status quo (*SQ*) or the initiative (*I*). Each player is assumed to have single peaked, symmetric preferences with ideal points *IG* and *V*, respectively.[11] This means that each player prefers policies that are closer to his or her ideal point to policies that are further away. The Interest Group first decides whether to expend resources to place an initiative on the ballot. If an initiative is proposed, the Interest Group expends additional

[10] For the current example, I assume there is only one interest group. I later consider the implications of a second interest group whose preferences conflict with those of the first. Because direct legislation voters choose between two policy alternatives, *SQ* and *I*, the median voter is decisive. Therefore, the Voter in this model represents the median voter in a large electorate.

[11] For ease of exposition, I further assume that player utility functions are linear, although this assumption is not critical.

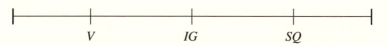

Fig. 2.1. Direct Influence Preference Configuration with Moderate Interest Group

resources to run a campaign. I assume these costs are fixed and known at the outset by the Interest Group. At the end of the campaign, the Voter chooses between the status quo (SQ) and the initiative (I).

The Interest Group can use the direct legislation process to achieve direct modifying influence if it can overcome the hurdles associated with placing a proposition on the ballot and can persuade the Voter to vote for the initiative. To get an idea of when these conditions are met, first consider the preference configuration illustrated in figure 2.1. In this figure, the Interest Group's ideal point is located between the Voter's ideal point and the status quo. Suppose the Interest Group proposes an initiative at its ideal point IG. Because the initiative I is closer to the Voter's ideal point than is SQ, the Voter prefers the initiative. In fact, whenever the Voter prefers the initiative to the status quo, the Interest Group only needs to mobilize sufficient resources to place the initiative on the ballot and run a minimal campaign.

When the Voter prefers the status quo to the initiative, however, as illustrated in figure 2.2, amassing majority support may be much more difficult. In

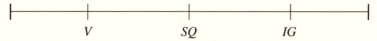

Fig. 2.2. Direct Influence Preference Configuration with Extreme Interest Group

addition to overcoming the hurdles associated with placing a measure on the ballot, the Interest Group must also expend enough resources to "move" the Voter away from its preelection ideal position. As explained in the discussion of campaign dynamics in chapter 3, moving the Voter's ideal point involves using a campaign to change the identity of the decisive voter in a given election. This is accomplished by providing information that leads some voters to switch their position from undecided or opposed to supportive or by inducing supporters to turn out in greater numbers.[12] The further the Voter's ideal point is from the initiative proposal, the more difficult moving this position will be and the more resources it will require. In this case, the Interest Group may be unable to achieve direct modifying influence, or it may have to propose an

---

[12] Note that this model does not require changing individual voters' primitive preferences over issues, but rather changing the identity of the voter who is decisive. An alternative view of campaigns that is easily subsumed into my framework actually involves using campaigns to change people's minds.

initiative so far from its ideal point that it can no longer justify the costs of making the proposal.

Suppose that there is a second Interest Group (with ideal point *IG2*) that opposes Interest Group 1's initiative proposal. Whether Interest Group 2 can achieve direct preserving influence depends again on the relative player preferences. Interest Group 2 can follow one of two strategies. The first is to run a competing campaign to oppose Interest Group 1's claims. This, in effect, raises Interest Group 1's costs of mobilizing an electoral majority (that is, of moving *V* closer to *I*) by introducing uncertainty and perhaps content information into the Voter's decision calculus (Gerber and Lupia 1995). The second strategy is to propose a competing initiative that splits off some voter support. This also has the effect of moving the position of the voter whose vote is decisive in the contest between the original initiative and the status quo.[13] Note that in either case, Interest Group 2 must prefer the status quo to the initiative.

Achieving Indirect Influence

Consider a group's ability to achieve indirect influence. To understand when a group can achieve indirect influence, we must also consider the presence of the state legislature. For simplicity, I represent the Legislature's preferences by an ideal point *LEG* and a linear, symmetric, single-peaked utility function. Although representing the Legislature as a unitary actor with a single ideal point obviously oversimplifies the complicated legislative process, consider *LEG* the point at which the Legislature, following its internal rules and procedures, would pass its policy on a given issue in the absence of other pressures (such as the threat of an initiative).[14]

To achieve indirect influence, the Interest Group must be able either (1) to threaten to propose and pass an adverse initiative, or (2) to use the initiative process to signal its preferences to the Legislature. For the Interest Group to achieve the second form of influence, its preferences and the Legislature's must be sufficiently aligned to make the Legislature willing to respond. Otherwise, the Legislature will simply find its support (financial and electoral) from other interest groups with more closely aligned preferences. When the Interest Group's preferences and the Legislature's preferences are similar, the Interest Group only needs to expend enough resources to attract the Legislature's attention and signal its preferences. Because the initiative need not receive majority support, the Voter's preferences are irrelevant. Note that in practice,

[13] For an analysis of "killer" initiatives, see Dubin et al. (1992).

[14] We can think of the Legislature's ideal point as reflecting the ideal point of the median legislator, or of the majority party's median member, or of some weighted average of legislator ideal points.

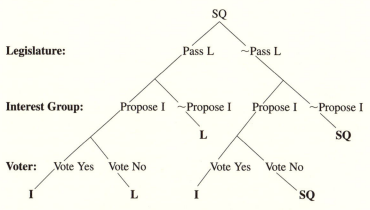

Fig. 2.3. Indirect Influence Sequence of Events

however, the Legislature may resist passing widely unpopular laws and therefore may be constrained to passing laws that are not too far from the Voter.[15]

For the Interest Group to achieve indirect influence by threatening an adverse initiative, the story becomes a bit more complicated. The game tree in figure 2.3 depicts the sequence of interaction among the Interest Group, the Voter, and the Legislature. The object of the game is again to select a single policy. The Legislature moves first and decides whether or not to pass a new law L. If the Legislature decides to act, it passes L through normal legislative channels. If the Legislature does not act, SQ is, in effect, the Legislature's chosen law. The underlying tension in this model is that the Legislature recognizes that some of its choices may provoke a challenging initiative. The Interest Group, in turn, recognizes that it may be able to influence what the Legislature does.

The Interest Group moves next and decides whether to propose an initiative. If no initiative is proposed, the game ends, and the Legislature's law (L or SQ) remains. If an initiative is proposed, then an election is held, and the Voter chooses whether the initiative (I) or the Legislature's law (L or SQ) prevails.

As in the previous versions of the model, the Interest Group's ability to pressure the Legislature depends in part on the configuration of player ideal points. Suppose the players' preferences are as depicted in figure 2.4. In this example, the Interest Group and the Voter have similar policy preferences,

---

[15] If the Interest Group's preferences are closely aligned with the Legislature's, one might ask why the group would choose to pressure the Legislature with an initiative instead of a more traditional lobbying strategy. On the one hand, signaling via an initiative campaign may be noisier than directly approaching legislators. On the other hand, there may be additional policy benefits from placing one's measure on the ballot (i.e., affecting public debate, setting the policy agenda) that are absent from a lobbying strategy. Undoubtedly, most groups would pursue indirect influence in conjunction with traditional lobbying.

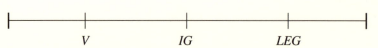

Fig. 2.4. Indirect Influence Preference Configuration with Moderate Interest Group

whereas the Legislature's policy preferences are relatively extreme.[16] If the Legislature and the Interest Group both proposed their ideal policies, then the initiative would win because the Voter would prefer the Interest Group's moderate policy $I = IG$ to the Legislature's extreme policy $L = LEG$. In this case, the Interest Group may be able to make a credible threat to the Legislature and force the Legislature to pass a law that it prefers.

Of course, the alignment of preferences is not the only factor that allows real-world interest groups to appear credible to real-world legislators. There is also the matter of getting a measure onto the ballot and running a successful campaign. Even if an interest group advocates a policy with broad public support, a legislator has no incentive to accede to the interest group's demands if he or she doubts that the group can actually qualify and pass the initiative. To show how this dynamic affects an interest group's ability to achieve indirect influence, let C (≥ 0) represent the cost of placing a winning initiative on the ballot.[17]

The general effect of these costs is as follows: As costs increase, the net benefits from using direct legislation decrease. As a result, as costs increase, the set of issues with which an Interest Group can threaten the Legislature decreases. I depict this situation in figure 2.5.

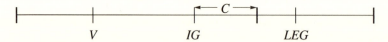

Fig. 2.5. Indirect Influence Preference Configuration with Moderate Interest Group, Proposer Costs $0 \leq C < |LEG - IG|$

In figure 2.5, when interest group costs $C = 0$, the Interest Group is willing and able to offer an initiative at its ideal point IG.[18] This initiative will beat any law that the Legislature prefers to I—that is, any point to the right of IG—because any such point is further from V than I is. Anticipating this, the Legis-

---

[16] Comparable results hold for the reverse case where $LEG < IG < V$.

[17] These costs include the costs of drafting, qualifying, campaigning for, and defending the initiative. I discuss these costs (hurdles) in chapter 3.

[18] Because the Interest Group (either alone or in coalition with other groups) must pay the costs of proposing, qualifying, and campaigning for the initiative, I assume the Interest Group must absorb these costs. By contrast, I assume the Legislature has already committed to considering policies in a given policy area, and therefore its costs are effectively zero. If I assume the Legislature must also absorb the costs (both direct costs and opportunity costs) of passing its law, the results extend straightforwardly.

lature knows the best it can do is pass its law at the Interest Group's ideal point *IG*. When *C* > 0, by contrast, if the Legislature passes a law close enough to *IG*, then the Interest Group will not find it cost-effective to propose an initiative. Therefore, the best that the Legislature can do in this example is to choose a law between *LEG* and *IG*, just close enough to *IG* to make the Interest Group indifferent between paying *C* and proposing an initiative and costlessly accepting the Legislature's proposal.[19] In this case, *L* is closer to the Legislature's ideal point than was true when *C* = 0. However, the Legislature's new proposal is further from the Voter's ideal point, implying that the decreased threat from the Interest Group made the Legislature less responsive to both the Interest Group and the Voter. Extending the logic of this example to the case where *C* is very large (i.e., when *LEG* and *IG* are less than *C* units apart), as in figure 2.6, the Legislature can do whatever it wants without fear of retribution from the Interest Group.[20]

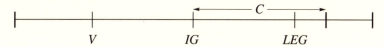

Fig. 2.6. Indirect Influence Preference Configuration with Moderate Interest Group, Proposer Costs $C \geq |LEG - IG|$

Fig. 2.7. Indirect Influence Preference Configuration with Extreme Interest Group

In figure 2.7, the Interest Group is also unable to achieve indirect influence by threatening the Legislature. This time, however, the reason has nothing to do with costs. In this case, the Legislature and the Voter have similar policy preferences, and it is the Interest Group that is extreme.[21] When player preferences are configured in this way, the Interest Group cannot propose any initiative that it and the Voter both prefer to the Legislature's ideal policy. Indeed, if the Interest Group proposes any initiative that is to the right of *L*, it will lose. Therefore, the Legislature passes its law at its ideal point *L* = *LEG* and ignores the Interest Group's potential threat.

To summarize, the legislature responds to an interest group's threat when the interest group can credibly threaten to propose an initiative that will garner

---

[19] Specifically, the Legislature passes its law *C* units from *IG*.

[20] When *LEG* < *V* < *IG* or *IG* < *V* < *LEG* and *C* = 0, the Legislature and the Interest Group each try to obtain the policy outcomes closest to their own ideal point, and both converge to the Voter's ideal point. When *C* > 0, the Legislature only needs to move *L* to the point that its law is a distance equal to half the Interest Group's costs. At that point, the Interest Group is willing to keep *C* and accept a policy *C* units from its best response on the other side of *V*.

[21] Comparable results hold for the reverse case in which *IG* < *LEG* < *V*.

majority support. If the interest group either supports policies that are unpopular with voters or lacks the resources to place a measure on the ballot and run a campaign, the interest group cannot gain indirect influence by threatening to pass an adverse initiative.

Summary and Conclusions

Groups promote their political interests by pursuing direct modifying, direct preserving, indirect modifying, or indirect preserving influence. The presence of direct legislation makes each of these four options available. Whether a group can use each of these options depends on whether it can overcome the hurdles associated with each form of influence. In particular, overcoming institutional hurdles requires mobilizing and expending certain combinations of monetary and personnel resources. The amount of resources necessary to overcome a particular set of hurdles depends on the behavioral hurdles created by the relationship among interest group, voter, and perhaps legislator preferences.

In the next chapter, I describe the institutional and behavioral hurdles that groups must overcome to achieve each form of influence. In chapter 4, I describe the resources groups can use to overcome these hurdles and generate a series of empirically testable hypotheses about the choices that groups with different internal characteristics will make.

3

Direct Legislation Hurdles

MY THIRD PREMISE is that the institutions of direct legislation and the regularities of voter behavior create hurdles that influence-seeking groups must overcome. These hurdles represent the effective costs of pursuing a group's policy goals through the direct legislation process.

To achieve their goals, groups choose particular strategies. A strategy is a plan of action that maps a group's goals to the actions required to achieve those goals. A strategy involves undertaking a particular set of political activities and entails overcoming a particular set of institutional and behavioral hurdles. Groups can choose among numerous strategies to achieve a given form of influence. For example, one strategy for achieving direct modifying influence involves proposing, qualifying, campaigning in support of, and defending an initiative. Because a group that pursues this strategy is responsible for all aspects of the measure at all stages of the process, it must overcome numerous hurdles. Other strategies require less extensive effort. A second strategy, for example, involves making a campaign contribution in favor of an existing initiative. Because they are not responsible for drafting or qualifying the measure, groups that undertake such a strategy would need to overcome only a subset of institutional and behavioral hurdles.

In this chapter, I describe some of the most common strategies that groups use to achieve each form of influence and the hurdles associated with those strategies. Based on extensive analysis of interest group activities and interviews with decision makers within numerous groups, I have identified thirteen common direct legislation strategies. This list takes account of the many ways that interest groups can and do use direct legislation to influence policy. I cannot claim that the list exhausts all of the possible direct legislation strategies groups may pursue, however. Rather, the list is empirically motivated, based on observed group strategies. Nor are the strategies I describe mutually exclusive. A group can and often does pursue several strategies simultaneously. What is important about these strategies is that they differ from those available to groups in states where direct legislation is not allowed. Table 3.1 lists the strategies that groups pursue to achieve each form of influence and the institutional hurdles associated with each strategy. Details follow in the text below.

TABLE 3.1
Direct Legislation Strategies and Institutional Hurdles

Form of Influence	Strategy	Hurdles[a]			
		Drafting	Qualifying	Campaign	Post-Election
Direct modifying	Propose initiative	X	X	X	X
	Form committee		X (I)[b]	X	
	Contribute to committee		X (I)[b]	X	
	Publicly endorse			X	
Direct preserving	Qualify popular referendum		X	X	X
	Propose competing initiative	X	X	X	
	Form committee			X	
	Contribute to committee			X	
	Legal challenge				X
Indirect modifying	Propose indirect initiative	X	X	X	X
	Propose direct initiative	X	X	X	
	Support initiative/submitted referendum		X (I)[b]	X	
Indirect preserving	Oppose initiative/submitted referendum			X	

[a] X indicates that a hurdle exists; a blank indicates that there is no hurdle.

[b] When groups form or contribute to committees to support initiatives, qualifying stage hurdles exist. When they form or contribute to committees to support submitted referendums, they do not exist.

Achieving Direct Modifying Influence

Achieving direct modifying influence through the direct legislation process involves passing a new law by initiative. To achieve direct modifying influence, a group can adopt one or more of the following strategies.

Strategy DM (Direct Modifying) 1: Proposing a Direct Initiative

Proposing a direct initiative involves drafting a measure and qualifying it for the ballot. In most cases, a group that proposes an initiative also runs a campaign in its favor and actively defends it against legislative amendments and legal challenges.

In states that allow direct initiatives, a group—either alone or in coalition with other supporters—can propose, qualify, campaign for, and defend a proposition by following a set of constitutionally mandated procedures. These procedures define the institutional hurdles that exist at four stages of the initiative process: the drafting stage; the qualifying stage; the campaign stage; and the postelection stage. Although these procedures vary from state to state, there are many common elements. I discuss the most important of these elements below. Differences in these hurdles across states are reported in Appendix A.

DRAFTING STAGE

The first step in proposing a direct initiative is drafting the proposition. Drafting represents a hurdle in the sense that a group that sponsors an initiative must organize, conduct research, and write the proposed legislation. Because states have few limitations on who can draft initiatives, initiative proposers can be any group of citizens. This includes both newly formed and previously established interest groups. It also includes government personnel acting in an unofficial capacity.[1] Drafting is frequently done with the help of legislators, professional consultants, or election officials such as the Secretary of State or the State Attorney General. Because drafting an initiative requires obtaining or paying for expertise, the hurdle at the drafting stage can be considerable for some groups.

Although few states have restrictions on who can draft initiatives, most limit an initiative's subject matter. Many states limit, restrict, or prohibit initiatives in the area of revenue and taxation. Several prohibit initiatives that affect the judiciary, and others prohibit initiatives that deal with emergency legislation. States commonly limit initiatives to a single subject and do not allow initiatives to name specific individuals or organizations.[2] Single-subject requirements are particularly interesting because they prohibit the kind of issue logrolling common in the U.S. Congress (Ferejohn 1974).

After the initiative has been drafted, most states require the proposer or sponsor to register with a state election official. The initiative is then submitted to the Secretary of State or State Attorney General. These officials review the initiative. They then provide an official title and summary or approve the title and summary supplied by the proposers.

QUALIFYING STAGE

Once the initiative is drafted, the proposer then begins the long and often very expensive task of qualifying the measure for the ballot. The usual qualification

[1] Several of the major recent initiatives in California were either written or sponsored by elected officials, acting as regular citizens, who used the initiative campaign to propel their own candidacies or political careers. Perhaps the most publicized recent examples are California Governor Pete Wilson's endorsement of Proposition 187 in 1994, the initiative that denied social services to illegal immigrants; Wilson's endorsement of Proposition 209 in 1996, the measure that prohibited California's affirmative action programs in public education, hiring, and contracting; and California's U.S. Senate candidate and multimillionaire Michael Huffington's endorsements of and contributions to several 1994 initiative campaigns.

[2] There is no consensus on what is meant by a "subject." Across jurisdictions, the single-subject requirement is unevenly enforced.

requirement is to collect a predetermined number of valid signatures from registered voters. The rationale behind signature requirements is to ensure that the initiatives that make it to the ballot have some public support. Most states set the signature requirement as a fixed percentage of the previous gubernatorial or other statewide election vote. Other states require a percentage of all registered voters or a percentage of the total state population. Signature requirements for constitutional initiatives are typically higher than signature requirements for statutory initiatives. The signature requirement ranges from 2 percent for statutory initiatives in North Dakota to 15 percent for both statutory and constitutional initiatives in Wyoming.[3] In 1996, the number of signatures required covered a broad range from 12,776 signatures to qualify statutory initiatives in North Dakota (North Dakota Secretary of State, Elections Department, telephone interview, 1997) to 693,230 signatures to qualify constitutional amendments in California (California Secretary of State, Elections Department, telephone interview, 1997). Thirteen states also have a geographic distribution requirement, mandating that signatures be collected from several counties, legislative districts, or regions of the state. In a very direct sense, as the number of required signatures increases, qualification hurdles become more difficult to clear.

One of the most controversial aspects of the initiative process in recent years has been the use of paid signature gatherers. Firms in several states provide petitioners who circulate petitions and qualify an initiative for a fee. The current rate in California is about $.70 per signature (Kimball Petition Management, telephone interview, 1997). Several states have attempted to prohibit the use of paid petitioners, requiring that volunteers gather signatures. In *Meyer v. Grant* (486 U.S. 414 [1988]), however, the U.S. Supreme Court ruled that such prohibitions are unconstitutional and violate the financers' First Amendment rights. Whether volunteers or professionals gather the signatures, signature requirements erect an important hurdle for initiative proposers.

All initiative states also have a limited circulation period during which the required number of signatures must be gathered and a deadline before the election by which the completed petitions must be submitted. After the signatures are gathered, the initiative proposer submits the petitions to a state election official for verification. The most common method for verification is a random check of some of the signatures with voter registration records. The possibility of fraud and the frequency of unregistered voters signing petitions mean that initiative proposers usually obtain extra signatures, sometimes up to 25 percent more than required.

If enough valid signatures are collected, then the initiative is placed on the next permissible ballot. Most states allow initiatives on general election ballots only, although several also allow them on primary and special election

---

[3] North Dakota requires 2 percent of the total resident population.

ballots. Once on the ballot, measures are usually listed in the order in which they qualify. Furthermore, signatures typically are not transferable from one circulation period to the next, so that if a group fails to obtain enough signatures, it must start over to qualify for a subsequent ballot. This time constraint makes the qualifying-stage hurdle even more difficult to clear.

CAMPAIGN STAGE

After drafting and qualifying the initiative, the next major phase is the campaign. The campaign actually may begin much earlier, during the drafting stage, while petitions are being circulated, or any time the group believes it has an opportunity to promote its position. Most groups wait until after their measure qualifies before they begin campaigning wholeheartedly, however. Campaign-stage hurdles affect a group's ability to use direct legislation because considerable resources are often required to run a successful campaign.[4] Institutional hurdles on the road to campaign success include disclosure requirements, restrictions on ballot placement and ballot order, majority requirements, and restrictions on contributions and expenditures.

Disclosure

All initiative states require individuals and/or groups who make contributions to initiative campaigns to report their activity.[5] To facilitate disclosure, groups establish campaign committees. Individuals and organizations contribute to committees, who then spend these resources on behalf of the campaign. These committees have legal status and are responsible for reporting contributions and expenditures. Campaign committees can be established either to support or to oppose an initiative. Several committees, on both sides of an issue, are often established to support and oppose a single initiative.

Typically, the submitted disclosure reports are publicly available but not widely distributed. Some critics of the direct legislation process argue that simply disclosing contributions and expenditures does not provide voters with sufficient information to understand who supports and opposes a given initiative (California Commission on Campaign Financing 1992). They contend that the true identity and interests of the groups that form committees to support or to oppose an initiative are often difficult to infer from committee names. In response, several states now require not only that the name of the sponsoring committee is identified but also that the names of the major group or groups providing funding for the committee are revealed.

---

[4] The success of a campaign depends on whether it allows the group to attain its desired policy outcome.

[5] Most states require disclosure of contributions over some dollar amount, ranging from $1 to $500.

Ballot Placement

A second institutional factor that affects the difficulty of running a successful campaign is the ballot on which the measure appears. Initiatives may be placed on primary, general, or special election ballots. Some states restrict initiatives to the general election. Because the composition of the electorate tends to be different in primary, general, and special elections, which ballot the initiative is on can affect the probability of success. For example, it may be easier for groups whose initiatives appeal to voters with relatively extreme preferences to run an effective campaign when they can place their initiatives on the ballots in primary or special elections.

Ballot Order

Ballot order may also be important. In most states, the initiatives are listed after the major candidate races. This means that fewer voters may actually cast votes on the initiatives as a result of ballot drop-off.[6] Magleby (1984) estimated as much as 15 percent ballot drop-off on some California statewide ballots. In other words, the number of voters casting votes for races lower on the ballot is 15 percent less than the number casting votes for the top race on the ballot. Magleby (1984) argued that voters who complete their ballots typically have different socioeconomic, demographic, and political characteristics than those who leave their ballots incomplete. These participation biases can affect the difficulty of running a successful campaign.

Majority Requirement

On election day, voters vote for or against the initiatives on the ballot. Registered voters may alternatively submit absentee ballots on or before election day. States typically require a simple majority of votes cast on a given initiative for it to pass, although some types of initiatives such as revenue or taxation measures may require a supermajority vote. Massachusetts requires that a constitutional initiative receive either 60 percent of the votes cast on the measure or 50 percent on two consecutive election ballots. In many states, if two or more competing propositions in a single issue area both pass, then the measure that receives the highest percentage of the vote prevails.[7] In such cases, the number of votes required for the initiative to take effect could be substantially higher than 50 percent. The higher the percentage of votes required, the more difficult it is for initiative sponsors to run a winning campaign.

[6] It is not entirely clear whether drop-off is due to voter fatigue and is therefore caused by placing propositions after candidates, or whether it is due to low levels of voter interest or information and is therefore unrelated to ballot order.

[7] In California, there have been times in recent years where competing initiatives both passed. The State Supreme Court ruled in *Taxpayers to Limit Campaign Spending v. FPPC* (51 Cal 3d. 744 [1990]) that in such situations only the measure that passed by the largest margin will be enforced. Procedures for dealing with competing initiatives in other states are less clearly delineated.

Contribution and Expenditure Restrictions

Perhaps the most striking feature of direct legislation campaigns is that contributions to and expenditures on such campaigns are unlimited. This is the case in every state that allows direct legislation at the statewide level. In contrast, presidential and congressional campaigns contain mandatory contribution limits; presidential campaigns also contain voluntary spending limits. In addition, many state candidate campaigns have contribution and expenditure limits.

The unlimited nature of direct legislation campaigns is the result of several U.S. Supreme Court decisions. In its landmark decision in *Buckley v. Valeo* (424 U.S. 1 [1976]), the court established basic principles with respect to the regulation of campaign financing. Although the decision considered the legality of the 1974 Amendments to the Federal Election Campaign Act and therefore strictly applied only to federal elections, many of the arguments made in *Buckley* laid the foundation for future court decisions that directly or indirectly addressed campaign financing in direct legislation campaigns.

In *Buckley*, the court upheld limits on contributions to candidate campaigns. The court argued that contributions to candidates were given to secure a political quid pro quo. Unlimited contributions could lead to corruption on the part of elected officials, whose campaign debts would lead them to compromise their principles in order to secure such contributions. Limits on contributions would therefore serve to reduce corruption, or at least the appearance of corruption, resulting from overreliance on large individual contributors. Thus, the court ruled that the abridgment of First Amendment rights could be justified. The court struck down all forms of expenditure limits, however, on the grounds that they impose direct and substantial restraints on the quantity of political speech without the benefit of reducing corruption.

With respect to spending limits in direct legislation campaigns, such expenditures are subject to the same reasoning that led the court to invalidate limits on spending in candidate campaigns in *Buckley*. These expenditures are considered expressions of speech protected by the First Amendment. With respect to contribution limits, however, the Supreme Court views candidate campaigns and direct legislation campaigns differently. In *First National Bank of Boston v. Bellotti* (435 U.S. 765 [1978]), the court established the right of corporations to make contributions to and expenditures on behalf of ballot measure campaigns. In its majority decision, the court argued that, contrary to prohibitions on contributions to candidate campaigns, where the potential for actual or perceived corruption associated with campaign contributions is great, the same corruptive potential does not exist in direct legislation. Following this line of argument, the court in *Citizens against Rent Control v. City of Berkeley* (454 U.S. 290 [1981]) reaffirmed prior decisions by further invalidating any limits on contributions to direct legislation committees. Again, the court deemed there was no potential for corruption, that is, no quid pro quo associated with these contributions that would justify the curtailment of First Amendment rights.[8]

After the election, opponents of an initiative may seek to amend the measure or challenge it in court. All states except California allow the state legislature to amend initiatives with a majority vote or, more typically, a supermajority vote.[9] Amendability is a hurdle in the sense that groups that want a particular policy outcome must defend their initiative from outcome-altering amendments after the election. In several states, legislative amendments are allowed for only some fixed period after passage of the initiative or require a supermajority vote. In California, an initiative can only be amended by another popular vote—a subsequent initiative or referendum—unless expressly permitted in the measure. This feature of the California initiative process makes laws that pass by its initiative process uniquely permanent.

Another hurdle for an initiative's sponsors is defending the initiative against (increasingly frequent) legal challenges in the state or federal court systems. The U.S. Supreme Court has broadly upheld citizens' rights to pass laws by initiative in states where direct legislation provisions exist. Federal courts typically do not differentiate between initiative and legislative laws.[10] State courts vary in their propensity to uphold laws passed by initiative. The hurdles associated with defending an initiative involve assembling expertise, defending the case, and financing the costs.[11]

The strategy of proposing an initiative allows an interest group to set the policy agenda directly. As Romer and Rosenthal (1978) proved, the agenda setter in a policy process such as the direct initiative can have substantial power to influence policy outcomes.[12] The interest group determines the content and

---

[8] Although several states have direct legislation contribution limits on the books, the legal decisions discussed above render them unconstitutional and unenforceable.

[9] Arizona prohibits postelection legislative amendments on initiatives that gain a vote equivalent to a majority of all registered voters in the state. To date, no Arizona initiative has achieved this level of support.

[10] A recent exception involves the Ninth Circuit Court decision on California's term limits initiative (Proposition 140) in which the court struck down the legislation on the grounds that voters did not understand the content of the legislation. At the time of this writing, the decision on term limits is currently being reviewed by the full Ninth Circuit.

[11] In some states, the attorney general, secretary of state, or other election official is largely responsible for defending initiative legislation. In other states, sponsoring groups play a greater role.

[12] Romer and Rosenthal model a process characterized by majority-rule voting between two

language of the proposition. In conjunction with state election officials, it selects the name and official description of the measure. It heads the effort to qualify the measure for the ballot and often coordinates the formation of a coalition of core supporters. It then leads the supporting coalition by coordinating fundraising and campaign efforts. Initiative proposers often provide substantial financial and nonfinancial resources to the initiative campaign. They are involved in defending their measure against postelection amendments and legal challenges as well.

Although the benefits of this strategy may be very high, the costs involved are also high. When groups propose initiatives to achieve direct modifying influence, they face substantial hurdles at each stage of the process. The proposing group must overcome the hurdles associated with drafting the measure, qualifying it for the ballot, running the campaign, mobilizing or persuading an electoral majority or supermajority, and protecting the measure against legislative and legal challenges. The costs of overcoming these hurdles are too high for many groups to absorb. For those that can overcome these numerous hurdles, however, the potential benefits that derive from setting the policy agenda and running the initiative campaign can be great.

Strategy DM2: Forming a Campaign Committee

A second strategy for achieving direct modifying influence involves forming a committee to support another group's initiative or submitted referendum.[13] Campaign committees allow individual groups to coordinate their resources in support of or in opposition to an existing ballot measure. Typically, the group that proposes an initiative forms a committee, and other groups have the option of either contributing to the initiative proposer's committee (see strategy DM3 below) or forming their own committee. One advantage to forming a separate committee is that the group retains control over how its funds are spent. In addition, by forming its own committee, a group may receive organizational benefits, such as experience, expertise, enhanced networks, and a larger resource base that it can draw upon in the future.

There are fewer hurdles associated with forming a campaign committee than with proposing an initiative. In the case of committees formed to support initiatives, no drafting stage hurdles exist because the measure has already been drafted. If the group forms the committee before the measure is qualified for

---

policy alternatives. The initiative process is perhaps the one actual policy process that most closely approximates the stylized process used by Romer and Rosenthal to illustrate their agenda-setting dynamics. In Romer and Rosenthal's model, whether the group can affect policy outcomes depends on the configuration of player ideal points and the existence of monopoly agenda power.

[13] Supporting an initiative or submitted referendum may lead to direct modifying influence by changing policy (whether placed on the ballot by petition or the legislature) through a popular vote.

the ballot, however, there may be hurdles associated with qualifying the measure. In the case of committees formed to support referendums submitted to the ballot by the legislature, no drafting or qualifying-stage hurdles exist because the legislature drafts the measure and places it on the ballot automatically.

In the later stages of the process, however, there are important institutional hurdles. When a group forms a campaign committee to help pass a new initiative or submitted referendum, the group and others in the supporting coalition must run a winning campaign. In addition, the group is responsible for disclosing the committee's contributions and expenditures and may be involved in the postelection stage. In other words, the campaign and postelection-stage hurdles are the same as those faced by groups that propose initiatives themselves.

Strategy DM3: Contributing to a Campaign Committee

A third strategy for achieving direct modifying influence involves contributing to an existing committee formed to support an initiative or submitted referendum. Contributors to campaign committees donate either financial or nonfinancial resources such as volunteers, office space, clerical support, and expertise. Contributions can range from a few dollars to millions of dollars. Whereas few groups use high-involvement strategies such as proposing an initiative, many make campaign contributions.

The hurdles associated with contributing to an existing committee are few. In the qualifying stage, groups face the same hurdles whether they form a committee or simply contribute to an existing committee: If the initiative is not already ballot qualified, supporters must raise and mobilize sufficient resources to place the measure on the ballot.[14] In the campaign stage, however, groups who merely contribute to existing committees face fewer hurdles because they are not responsible for disclosure. In addition, most groups whose involvement is limited to contributing to a supporting committee are not involved in the postelection stage.

Strategy DM4: Publicly Endorsing an Initiative or Referendum

A fourth strategy involves publicly endorsing a ballot measure. Groups may endorse ballot measures either during the qualifying stage (for initiatives) or, more commonly, during the campaign stage. Some endorsements convey a great deal of information to voters about the content and likely consequences of the measure; others are less informative. The informative value of an endorsement depends largely on the characteristics of the group making the en-

---

[14] Again, in the case of submitted referendums, there are no qualifying-stage hurdles.

dorsement, such as whether their policy positions are well known (Lupia 1994). It also depends on characteristics of the environment in which these groups make their endorsement, such as whether the endorser's reputation is at stake (Lupia and McCubbins 1998).

Endorsing a measure entails even less of a resource commitment than forming or contributing to a campaign committee. The endorsing group simply makes a statement in favor of the measure. There are no drafting, qualifying, or postelection hurdles associated with an endorsement strategy. The hurdles associated with the campaign stage are comparable to those in the other direct modifying strategies, requiring a sufficiently vigorous campaign to obtain a majority vote in favor of the initiative or referendum. The benefits from endorsing an existing initiative or referendum proposition may also be low, however, because the endorser rarely has any control over the policy agenda.

Achieving Direct Preserving Influence

Achieving direct preserving influence through the direct legislation process involves repealing legislation through a popular referendum or blocking passage of a new law by initiative. To achieve direct preserving influence by either of these methods, a group can adopt the following strategies.

Strategy DP (Direct Preserving) 1: Qualifying a Popular Referendum

One strategy for preserving or protecting the status quo is qualifying a popular referendum. In the popular referendum, the legislature passes a law, and an interest group petitions to have the law placed on the ballot for voter approval. Whereas initiatives are typically used to change policy proactively, popular referendums are used in response to unfavorable legislation. That is, the intention of a popular referendum is to revert policy back to the preexisting status quo.

Winning a popular referendum involves heading the petition drive to have a legislative measure placed on the ballot and running a successful campaign.[15] In the drafting stage of the referendum process—both popular and submitted—the legislature drafts the measure and interest groups therefore face minimal hurdles.[16] In the qualifying stage, the hurdles associated with the popular

[15] As with strategy DM1 (proposing a direct initiative), a group could, in theory, lead the effort to qualify a referendum but not play an important role in the campaign. In practice, this is extremely rare.

[16] In both the popular and submitted referendum, interest groups may lobby legislators while the legislation is being drafted. These drafting-stage hurdles, however, are quite different from those associated with the initiative process where the group writes the legislation itself.

referendum are substantial. The qualification procedure is similar to qualifying an initiative: The group registers with a state election official; receives and circulates petitions; and obtains a fixed number of signatures.

In the campaign stage, groups pursuing this strategy face important hurdles, because they must mobilize a statewide majority for the referendum (i.e., against the legislature's measure). Note that the referendum's proponents have a task different from that of an initiative's proponents because they must mobilize a majority to oppose, rather than support, a change to the status quo.[17]

Groups employing this strategy have an important influence over the policy agenda by determining which measures will be on the ballot. They do not set the policy agenda unilaterally, however, because the referendum is, by definition, an election to ratify or reject a measure already passed by the legislature.

Strategy DP2: Proposing a Competing Initiative

A second strategy for preserving the status quo is proposing an initiative to block passage of another initiative. When a group proposes a competing or "killer" initiative, the dynamics are a bit complicated. The logic behind proposing a competing initiative is to draw support away from other measures on the ballot. For example, if a group opposes an extreme initiative, it can place a more moderate alternative on the ballot and attract the support of moderate voters who prefer the extreme initiative to the status quo but also prefer the moderate alternative to the extreme initiative. The point of a competing or killer initiative is not necessarily to pass the moderate alternative but rather to use it to kill support for the extreme measure.[18]

The hurdles associated with proposing a competing initiative are important at the drafting, qualifying, and campaign stages of the direct legislation process. During the drafting and qualifying stages, they are comparable to proposing a regular initiative. In the campaign stage, the group must run a sufficiently vigorous campaign to reduce to less than a majority the support for the measure it opposes. Finally, groups who pursue direct preserving influence by

---

[17] I discuss the differences between passing and defeating a change to the status quo in the section on campaign hurdles below.

[18] A group's ability to use competing initiatives in this way depends on how voters evaluate the several alternatives and on the rules used when several competing initiatives pass. If voters vote only for the measure closest to their ideal points, then this strategy can be effective because support is split between the two alternative propositions. If, however, voters vote for any measure they prefer to the status quo, the ability to protect the status quo with a killer initiative depends on several factors. These factors include the distribution of preferences and the locations of the several measures and the status quo (see Dubin et al. 1992). Regarding counting rules, the California State Supreme Court ruled in *Taxpayers to Limit Campaign Spending v. FPPC* (51 Cal 3d. 744 [1990]) that if two competing measures both pass, only the measure that receives the greatest number of votes becomes law. This ruling works in favor of groups who use competing initiatives to protect the status quo because the measure they oppose only becomes law if it passes by the greater number of votes. Other states have yet to establish such procedures.

proposing competing initiatives need not concern themselves with protecting their measure in the postelection stage because their purpose is to defeat the measure they oppose rather than pass the measure they propose.

Strategy DP3: Forming a Campaign Committee

As with strategy DM2 (forming a supporting campaign committee) above, groups may also form campaign committees to oppose initiatives or submitted referendums or to support popular referendums. All are aimed at achieving direct preserving influence in the sense that they oppose a change to the status quo. Forming a committee allows a group to pool its resources with other like-minded groups. It may result in some organizational benefits to the group, especially in terms of developing networks and ongoing coalitions with other contributors, and allows the group some control over how its resources are spent.

The hurdles associated with forming a campaign committee to oppose an initiative or submitted referendum occur primarily at the campaign stage because the group's efforts, in coalition with others, are aimed at mobilizing a statewide majority against the measure. They may also occur at the postelection stage if the measure passes and the committee is involved in the subsequent legislative or legal challenge. The hurdles associated with forming a committee to support a popular referendum may also occur at the qualifying stage if the measure is not yet qualified for the ballot.

Strategy DP4: Contributing to a Campaign Committee

Likewise, the hurdles associated with contributing to an existing campaign committee to oppose an initiative or submitted referendum or to support a popular referendum are analogous to those associated with contributing to a committee formed to support a change in the status quo. The campaign-stage hurdles are fewer than those associated with forming such a committee (strategy DP3 above) because the contributor is not responsible for disclosure. Hurdles rarely occur at the postelection stage because groups whose involvement is limited to contributing to an existing committee are rarely involved in the postelection amendment process.

Strategy DP5: Challenging a Direct Legislation Law in Court

A fifth strategy aimed at direct preserving influence is coordinating a legal challenge to a law passed by direct legislation. Many laws passed by direct legislation now face legal challenges (California Commission on Campaign

Financing 1992). These challenges may be on procedural, administrative, or constitutional grounds. The hurdles associated with coordinating the legal challenge against a measure involve bringing a suit, assembling expertise, litigating the case, and financing the costs. The hurdles associated with defending an initiative against a legal challenge may be lower because the state covers some of the costs of defending laws that pass as initiatives.[19]

Achieving Indirect Modifying Influence

Achieving indirect modifying influence involves using the direct legislation process to pressure other actors to change policy. Groups can pursue indirect modifying influence by proposing an indirect initiative or by proposing or supporting a direct initiative to signal the legislature.

Strategy IM (Indirect Modifying) 1: Proposing an Indirect Initiative

A first strategy for pursuing indirect modifying influence is proposing an indirect initiative. In states that allow indirect initiatives, proposers draft the measure, collect the required number of signatures, and present the qualified initiative to the legislature. If the legislature passes the measure as it is written, then it becomes law. If the legislature fails to pass the measure, then it is placed on the ballot as an initiative. Legislative involvement in the indirect initiative, compared to that in the direct initiative, can lower the institutional hurdles faced by groups who want to use the direct legislation process to influence policy.

Proposers draft propositions as in the direct initiative. In some states, qualification requirements are the same for direct and indirect initiatives; in other states, the signature requirement for indirect initiatives is lower. In either case, once the required number of signatures is collected and verified, the legislature holds hearings on the measure. Depending on the state's provisions, the hearings may be mandatory, at the legislature's option, or at the proposer's (sponsor's) option.

After the required signatures are gathered and the necessary hearings held, legislators vote on the proposition. In some states, legislators are required to register a floor vote on all qualified indirect initiatives. In others, a legislative committee or appointed commission first votes on whether to send the bill to the floor.

[19] Once a law passes as an initiative (or as regular legislation), it becomes official state policy, and the state takes the responsibility for defending the law against legal challenges. Typically, the initiative's original proposers and other parties are also involved in the defense.

The ability of state legislatures to revise or amend the measures they consider varies substantially. Some state legislatures are permitted to vote only on the original proposal. Others are able to make minor revisions that are consistent with the original intent and purpose of the initiative proposal. Still others are able to amend the original proposal drastically.

In most states that offer the indirect initiative, the measure is automatically placed on the ballot if the legislature fails to approve it. In some states such as Massachusetts, however, the proposer is required to obtain additional signatures before the measure is placed on the ballot.

If the legislature approves the measure, there is still a question of whether the initiative will be placed on the ballot. In some states, the proposition is automatically removed from the ballot after approval by the legislature, whereas in other states, it is removed only at the request of the initiative proposer. Because amending a law passed by initiative is more difficult in some states than amending a law passed by a legislature, groups may have an extra incentive to place their preferred policy on the ballot. By passing the law as an initiative, the measure may be better protected against repeal or amendment.

Note that if the legislature passes an indirect initiative, the hurdles on the road to influence are lower than the hurdles associated with the direct initiative. Groups still need to overcome hurdles at the drafting and qualifying stages, but they may be able to influence policy without running a costly campaign. In other words, there may be few campaign-stage hurdles. If the legislature does not pass the measure, then the institutions that define the campaign and postelection stages of the indirect initiative process are identical to those of the direct initiative process.

Strategy IM2: Proposing an Initiative to Signal the Legislature

A second strategy for achieving indirect modifying influence involves proposing an initiative to signal the legislature. As discussed in chapter 2, groups may be able to persuade the state legislature to pass a law they support if they can either signal convergent preferences to the legislature or credibly threaten to pass an initiative the legislature opposes.

When groups propose initiatives to signal the legislature, they potentially face the same drafting and qualifying hurdles as when they propose initiatives with the intention of passing the law (strategy DM1). They may also have to overcome campaign-stage hurdles to make their positions known. Depending on the nature of uncertainty, however, the legislature may pick up the group's signal without a full-fledged qualifying effort and campaign, sparing the group the need to overcome these hurdles.

Strategy IM3: Contributing to an Initiative Committee

Groups may also contribute to committees for an existing initiative to signal their preferences to the legislature. The hurdles associated with this strategy may be important at the qualifying stage if the measure is not already qualified and at the campaign stage if the legislature is sufficiently uncertain about the group's signal that it must observe a costly campaign.

Achieving Indirect Preserving Influence: Opposing an Initiative to Signal the Legislature

Achieving indirect preserving influence involves opposing an initiative to signal the group's preferences to the legislature. As in strategy IM3 (contributing to an initiative committee) above, the hurdles associated with the campaign stage depend on whether the legislature is sufficiently uncertain about the group's signal that it must observe a costly campaign to infer the group's preferences. As in strategy IM3 above, no drafting, qualifying, or postelection hurdles are associated with this strategy.

Behavioral Hurdles

Institutional hurdles only partially determine the dynamics of interest group involvement in the direct legislation process. The conduct of other actors, including the behavior of voters and other interest groups, can affect the difficulty of overcoming hurdles. These dynamics are particularly important at the campaign stage of the direct legislation process. In the following section, I first consider how other groups, especially opposing interest groups, can affect the difficulty of overcoming direct legislation hurdles at the campaign stage. I then consider how voters further affect the difficulty of overcoming campaign-stage hurdles.

Campaign Hurdles

The difficulty of overcoming campaign-stage hurdles is determined first and foremost by the competitiveness of the campaign. The proponents' and opponents' decisions together influence how competitive an initiative or referendum campaign will be.

I say that direct legislation campaigns are competitive when interest groups on both sides of an issue organize, mobilize resources, and dedicate those resources to pursuing a direct legislation strategy. Competitive campaigns most often occur on controversial moral or social issues such as gay rights, affirmative action, and immigration policy. On these issues, both sides feel intensely about the matter. They have much to gain if their side prevails and much to lose if their side fails.

By contrast, noncompetitive campaigns most often concern regulatory issues about which only one side feels intensely. On these issues, the costs of a new policy are diffuse, whereas the benefits are concentrated or the benefits are diffuse but the costs are concentrated (see Lowi 1972). For example, some of the most expensive recent noncompetitive campaigns involved insurance initiatives in California and Michigan. These issues pitted the insurance industry and/or trial lawyers against regulators, in particular, and certain consumers, more generally. Clearly, the insurance industry and trial lawyers had much at stake. The costs and benefits to consumers, by contrast, were much more diffuse. Other noncompetitive campaigns occur when neither side of an issue feels intensely. These small, noncompetitive campaigns are most common on submitted referendums that deal with mundane procedural issues.

Competition affects the height of campaign-stage hurdles by influencing the amount of effort required to run a winning campaign. The effects of competition in direct legislation campaigns parallel the effects of competition on profit-maximizing firms by lowering the profitability of some political strategies. In economics, competitiveness drives down the prices that firms can charge for their goods. Thus, a firm receives less profit from a given mode of production when the market is competitive. Competition in direct legislation campaigns also drives down "profits." However, competition in direct legislation campaigns tends to affect the costs rather than the benefits of political activity. Competition forces groups to allocate scarce resources toward countering their opponents' claims and accusations. Thus, for a given political strategy to be victorious, interest groups in competitive campaigns must spend more resources than they would if the campaign were not competitive.

In addition to forcing proponents to address the claims made by opponents, competition increases the amount of effort required to run a winning campaign in other ways as well. Most important, competition may make voters harder to manipulate. Recall that in market settings, competition limits the ability of any one actor to influence unilaterally the outcome of a market transaction. Gerber and Lupia (1995) applied the logic of microeconomics and signaling theory to explore the applicability of this point to direct legislation elections. They found that campaign competition improves voters' ability to cast votes that are consistent with their interests when competition enhances the credibility of the campaigners.[20] To the extent that increased competition sharpens

---

[20] For example, when voters observe a campaigner spending scarce resources to affect an electoral outcome, they can infer that the campaigner believes the ballot measure will make him or her sufficiently better off, compared to the status quo, to justify the expenditure. Otherwise, the

voter inferences, groups whose ability to influence policy depends on their ability to manipulate public opinion will face higher hurdles at the campaign stage.

Electoral Hurdles

The difficulty of overcoming campaign-stage hurdles depends not only on the amount of competition a group faces; it also depends critically on the underlying electoral support for the measure. In particular, campaigns may be designed either to mobilize latent support for a measure or to generate support that did not previously exist. Each of these campaign objectives—mobilization and persuasion—corresponds to a view of campaign effects common in the political science literature. I argue that both mobilization and persuasion are important in direct legislation campaigns. The extent to which influence requires mobilization or persuasion determines the height of the campaign-stage hurdles.

MOBILIZATION

A *mobilization campaign* is one in which the group managing a campaign seeks to tap into existing support for a measure. Mobilization is consistent with the view of campaigns common in the formal theory literature.[21] According to this view, campaigns help voters link their known and fixed preferences with the policy alternatives. Campaigns do little more than provide voters with the information they need to act on their preexisting preferences. Seen from this perspective, campaigns are not used to manipulate or persuade; rather, they help voters better understand the relationship between their own preferences and their policy choices.

For proponents of ballot propositions, mobilization is important when public opinion is already favorably predisposed toward the group's policy goals. In the language of the spatial model presented in chapter 2, mobilization is important when the median voter's precampaign ideal point is closer to the group's ideal point than it is to the status quo. Mobilization is also important on controversial issues such as abortion or capital punishment where

---

campaigner would simply keep the resources and accept the status quo policy. Therefore, when voters observe campaign activity, they can infer that the ballot measure is at least some distance from the status quo, and they can update their beliefs about the location of the ballot measure based on this new information. Gerber and Lupia (1995) also found that competition creates incentives to be more truthful. The key factor here is the adversarial nature of competitive campaigns. Campaigners cannot lie as easily when there is an opponent who has an interest in pointing out the other campaigner's lies.

[21] See Spence (1973), Crawford and Sobel (1982), and Lupia (1992) on the use of costly signals.

opinions are already well formed. On these hot-button issues, few voters are likely to change their minds in the course of a direct legislation campaign. In other words, it may be very difficult to move the median voter's position through campaign activity. The most a group can hope to achieve through its campaign is to draw attention to what is at stake in the election and to bring out its supporters. Consequently, in campaigns in which the electorate has already formed firm opinions, the difficulty of overcoming campaign-stage hurdles depends on how favorable preexisting opinion is to the group's policy position.

PERSUASION

A persuasion campaign is one in which the group managing a campaign seeks to change voters' opinions about a particular issue. In a persuasion campaign, voters learn not just how the electoral alternatives map into their own pre-existing preferences but also about the nature of their preferences. Campaigns affect which issues voters consider important (i.e., framing or agenda setting), how they view the political alternatives, and how they perceive their own interests.

Persuasion is, all else constant, more difficult than mobilization because it involves generating electoral support that did not already exist. In other words, persuasion requires changing the way people view the issues and the relation-ship between the issues and their preferences. A group that must use a campaign to persuade voters therefore faces a higher campaign-stage hurdle than one that must simply mobilize preexisting support. We would expect persuasion to be most effective on new issues (because voters' opinions are only beginning to develop) and on mundane issues that are of low salience to voters.

Evidence from direct legislation campaigns shows that the ability of campaigns to persuade voters to support a measure that they did not previously support is limited at best. First, very few campaigns that begin with low voter support eventually win. California's Field Polls provide ample evidence of the difficulty that groups have in persuading voters. From 1990 to 1996, the Field Poll measured initial support for fifty-eight California statewide ballot propositions by periodically polling registered and/or likely voters several months before the election (DiCamillo and Field 1990–1996). Only six of the fifty-eight measures passed without receiving the support of a majority of respondents in at least one preelection poll. By contrast, thirty-two measures received majority support in at least one of the early polls, but only thirteen of the thirty-two ultimately passed. This evidence suggests that a majority of voters can rarely be persuaded to support a measure it did not favor at the beginning of a campaign, although they may be persuaded through a campaign to oppose a measure.

Second, not only do ballot measures rarely pick up enough support during the campaign to win, but also aggregate support for measures almost never increases over the course of a campaign. Again, evidence for this point is drawn from Field Poll data. Of the fifty-eight propositions on which the Field Poll measured preelection voter support from 1990 to 1996, only three times did aggregate support increase by more than five percentage points. Thus, on basis of aggregate preference data, there is little evidence of successful persuasion in favor of recent ballot propositions.

UNCERTAINTY

In addition to underlying voter support, the risk voters perceive to be associated with a given choice may affect the difficulty of overcoming campaign-stage hurdles. There is an inherent asymmetry in the decisions that voters make in direct legislation elections. This asymmetry has to do with the differential risk of voting for or against a proposition. When voters vote against a ballot measure, they are voting for the status quo. Even if they are largely unaware of the content of the current status quo policy, voters have lived under the status quo and have experienced its effects. A proposed change in the status quo, by contrast, engenders much more uncertainty. Even the most knowledgeable experts can only speculate as to the consequences of a new policy. Regular voters are likely to have even less substantive information about the future consequences of a new policy.

If voters are risk neutral, they simply incorporate the greater uncertainty of the ballot measure into their evaluation of the two policy outcomes and vote accordingly. If voters are risk averse, by contrast, they may favor the status quo, even if the preponderance of campaign information suggests that they should do otherwise. Independent of other mobilization or persuasion campaign effects, risk aversion leads to a bias in voting toward the status quo.

One consequence of voter risk aversion is that if campaigners expect voters to behave this way, opponents of direct legislation propositions may design their campaigns to emphasize and cultivate uncertainty about a proposition, even further biasing voters' tendencies to favor the status quo. This risk aversion may also give a measure's opponents an additional advantage because they only need to generate sufficient uncertainty about any one aspect of a proposition to defeat the entire measure, whereas proponents must mitigate concerns about all aspects of the measure.

Overcoming Campaign Stage Hurdles

These regularities of campaign dynamics and voter decision making have important implications for interest groups pursuing direct legislation strategies. Specifically, they imply systematic differences in the difficulty of overcoming

TABLE 3.2
Comparison of Campaign Stage Hurdles

Form of Influence	Campaign Stage Hurdle	Comparison between Campaign Stage Hurdles for Two Forms of Influence
Direct modifying	majority support	high
Direct Preserving	majority oppose	equal or lower
Direct (modifying or preserving)	majority support	high or medium
Indirect (modifying or preserving)	≤ majority support	equal or lower
Indirect modifying	signal support	??
Indirect preserving	signal opposition	??

the campaign-stage hurdles associated with strategies aimed at each of the four forms of influence. Table 3.2 summarizes these regularities.

The first two rows of table 3.2 compare the campaign-stage hurdles associated with pursuing direct modifying and direct preserving influence. Direct modifying influence involves mobilizing or persuading a statewide majority to *accept* a change to the status quo. Direct preserving influence, by contrast, requires mobilizing or persuading a statewide majority to *oppose* a change to the status quo. As discussed in the section on uncertainty above, if voters are risk averse, then there will be a bias in favor of the status quo.[22] There is some evidence in the literature that the risk-aversion hypothesis applies to voting on initiatives and referendums. For example, aggregate election returns suggest that campaigns against ballot measures are more successful than campaigns for ballot measures (Lowenstein 1982; Owens and Wade 1986). In addition, analysis of survey data by Bowler and Donovan (1998) provides some evidence of risk aversion because voters tend to vote "no" when they are uncertain. To the extent that voters are risk averse, then all else constant, it will be more difficult to mobilize a majority in favor of a change to the status quo. To the extent that voters are risk neutral, it will be equally difficult to mobilize a majority in favor or against the status quo. Therefore, the campaign-stage hurdles associated with direct preserving influence are lower than or equal to the campaign-stage hurdles associated with direct modifying influence.

The middle two rows of table 3.2 compare the campaign-stage hurdles associated with direct versus indirect influence. Direct modifying or preserving influence requires mobilizing or persuading a statewide majority to accept or

[22] If voters are risk acceptant, they will prefer the unknown policy in the initiative proposal. However, there is little theoretical or empirical justification for voter risk acceptance in political decision making. I therefore assume that voters are not risk acceptant in their voting decisions. This assumption is consistent with the standard view of voter decision making in political science.

reject, respectively, a change to the status quo. Indirect influence requires persuading the state legislature to accept or reject a change to the status quo by
signaling the group's preference. Indirect influence may require the support of
substantially less than an electoral majority to signal the legislature effectively.
At a minimum, it should never require more than an electoral majority because
a group that can amass an electoral majority in support of its position can
achieve its policy goals directly and need not rely on the legislature. Therefore,
all else constant, indirect influence entails identical or lower campaign-stage
hurdles than direct influence.

The last two rows of table 3.2 indicate that, although one might like to
compare the campaign-stage hurdles associated with the two forms of indirect
influence, the differences are likely to be the result of features of the *legislative*
process, not of the *direct legislation* process. Therefore, a comparison of the
campaign-stage hurdles associated with the indirect forms of influence is be-
yond the focus of the current analysis.

Summary and Conclusions

Embedded within each direct legislation strategy is a unique combination of
institutional and behavioral hurdles. Interest groups must overcome these hurdles if they are to use a strategy to influence policy. Furthermore, the level of
some hurdles varies according to the form of influence the group pursues.
Most importantly, campaign-stage hurdles vary, depending on whether the
group wishes to pass legislation, block legislation, or pressure other actors.

Groups need certain types of resources to overcome the hurdles embodied
in each strategy. In the next chapter, I consider the types of resources different
groups are able to amass. I argue that internal characteristics largely determine
a group's comparative advantage at mobilizing the several types of resources.
Therefore, because economic groups and citizen groups have different internal
characteristics, they can amass different kinds of resources. Ultimately, this
means that they are likely to pursue different strategies and to achieve different
forms of influence. I end the chapter with a set of hypotheses about the strategies and forms of influence different groups are likely to pursue.

4

Group Characteristics and Resources

MY FOURTH PREMISE is that groups need particular resources to clear the hurdles associated with a given direct legislation strategy. These resources include monetary resources such as cash and other financial assets, and personnel resources such as members, volunteers, and experts.

I begin this chapter with a discussion of the monetary and personnel resources required at each stage of the direct legislation process. I then consider the conditions under which groups can mobilize monetary and personnel resources. My fifth premise is that interest groups vary in the resources they are able to mobilize. I describe how a group's characteristics translate into a comparative advantage at mobilizing each type of resource. I then use this explanation to identify the likely resource bases of the most common participants in direct legislation elections, including economic groups and citizen groups. I end the chapter by generating a set of empirically testable hypotheses about the strategies and forms of influence that groups with different internal characteristics will pursue.

Monetary and Personnel Resources

Groups can employ two types of resources; monetary and personnel.[1] Monetary resources include money and other financial assets. Monetary resources come primarily from dues paid by members and from grants and gifts donated by government, foundations, and private citizens (Walker 1991). They can also come from sales of merchandise, proceeds from conventions, and income from investments. A group's monetary resources are akin to a firm's supply of capital.

Personnel resources are the manpower resources that derive directly from a group's membership, including volunteers, experts, and others from within the group whose skills can be used to overcome direct legislation hurdles. A group's personnel resources are akin to a firm's supply of labor.

---

[1] Organizational resources are a third type of resource. Groups with abundant organizational resources have fancy offices; large professional staffs; state or local chapters with well-developed communication networks; extensive mailing lists, etc. These resources allow the group to mobilize its monetary or personnel resources more effectively. Organizational resources are secondary to our analysis, however, in the sense that they neither derive from a group's internal characteristics nor directly affect a group's choice of strategy.

Using Resources to Overcome Hurdles

Groups can employ monetary and personnel resources to overcome the hurdles associated with a given direct legislation strategy. Table 4.1 identifies the resources required to overcome hurdles at each stage of the direct legislation process.

Drafting Stage

When groups propose initiatives, they face important drafting-stage hurdles. Groups must write a law that is technically sound and complies with any restrictions on content. Provisions that affect the height of the drafting-stage hurdles include single-subject laws and other content restrictions. To clear drafting-stage hurdles, groups require personnel resources in the form of experts to draft their proposition or monetary resources to hire experts from outside the group.

Qualifying Stage

Whenever groups propose initiatives or popular referendums, they face qualifying-stage hurdles. When they support existing initiatives or referendums, they may also face qualifying-stage hurdles if the measure has not yet qualified for the ballot. To qualify direct initiatives, indirect initiatives, and popular referendums, groups must gather signatures. Factors that affect the height of the qualifying-stage hurdles include the signature requirement, restrictions on paid signatures, length of the circulation period, and qualification deadline. To overcome these hurdles, groups must expend either personnel resources in the form of volunteer petition circulators or monetary resources to pay professional signature gatherers. In the qualifying stage of the submitted referendum, by contrast, the legislature places the measure on the ballot automatically, so that no interest group resources are required at this stage.[2]

Campaign Stage

When groups undertake any of the thirteen strategies except posing a legal challenge, they face campaign-stage hurdles. Groups must raise money and

---

[2] As described in chapter 3, a group may lobby the legislature to place a submitted referendum on the ballot. However, this qualifying-stage hurdle is voluntary in the sense that the group's effort is not formally required to place the measure on the ballot.

TABLE 4.1
Direct Legislation Strategies and Resources

Form of Influence	Strategy	Resources[a]			
		Drafting	Qualifying	Campaign	Post-election
Direct modifying	Propose initiative	M or P	M or P	M and P	M or P
	Form committee		M or P	M and P	
	Contribute to committee		M or P	M and P	
	Publicly endorse			M and P	
Direct preserving	Qualify popular referendum		M or P	M or P	M or P
	Propose competing initiative	M or P	M or P	M or P	
	Form committee			M or P	
	Contribute to committee			M or P	
	Legal challenge				M or P
Indirect modifying	Propose indirect initiative	M or P	M or P	M or P	M or P
	Propose direct initiative	M or P	M or P	M or P	
	Support initiative/submitted referendum		M or P	M or P	
Indirect preserving	Oppose initiative/submitted referendum			M or P	

[a] M, monetary; P, personnel.

other resources, run a campaign, and disclose contributions to and expenditures by their campaign committees. Institutional factors that affect the height of the campaign-stage hurdles include campaign finance laws, restrictions on ballot placement and order, majority requirements, and disclosure requirements. Other factors that affect the height of the campaign-stage hurdles include competition from other interest groups and voter behavior.

Some of these campaign-stage hurdles may be overcome using personnel resources. For example, volunteers run fundraisers, stage demonstrations and rallies, canvas their local communities, and engage in other forms of grassroots campaigning. Personnel also make public endorsements. Historically, these forms of personnel-intensive campaign activities were the mainstays of direct legislation campaigns. Recent technological changes in the nature of political campaigns, however, have rendered such grassroots campaign activities insufficient for modern statewide ballot measure campaigns. The dominance of television, radio, direct mail, and other forms of expensive paid political advertising means that in large (statewide) electorates, groups in even small states simply cannot compete effectively for voter attention with traditional grassroots forms of campaigning. In virtually all modern direct legislation campaigns, whether or not groups engage in personnel-intensive campaigning, they must spend substantial monetary resources to purchase campaign advertisements.[3]

Though monetary resources are necessary to run an effective media-intensive statewide direct legislation campaign, they may not be sufficient. Whether they are sufficient depends on what form(s) of influence the group hopes to achieve. When a group's goal is to preserve the status quo or to pressure the legislature, monetary resources may be sufficient. When pressuring the legislature, groups may be able to signal their preferences by spending monetary resources on direct legislation activities. Whether these resources are sufficient depends on whether groups can spend enough to attract the attention of important legislators and whether those legislators view the groups as important constituents. When attempting to preserve the status quo, groups simply need to create enough doubt and concern about the measure to dissuade a majority of the electorate from supporting the new policy. Bombarding voters with paid campaign advertisements that promise horrible consequences if the measure passes, even if the messages contained in these ads are barely believable, may be enough to create sufficient concern. Especially when voters are risk averse, groups that expend large amounts of monetary resources may be able to convince enough voters that the known status quo policy, although perhaps not optimal, is preferable to the risky, unknown alternative policy.[4]

When, on the other hand, the goal is to pass a new initiative, monetary resources are simply not enough, for two reasons. The first reason relates to the many activities groups must engage in to pass a new law. Mobilizing or persuading a statewide electoral majority to support an initiative requires mobilizing a vast array of diverse interests, building networks with other groups, fundraising, and coordinating numerous campaign-related activities. It is very difficult to pay someone to undertake all of these activities on behalf of a direct legislation campaign. In particular, even though groups may pay consultants to manage most aspects of their direct legislation campaigns, those consultants have few incentives to establish vital long-term contacts with other groups and to engage in other coalition-building activities that may be critical to the measure's success. A related point is that when groups can use their own personnel resources to undertake the coalition-building and other organizational activities mentioned above, they gain flexibility to use whatever monetary resources they are able to mobilize to purchase advertisements. By contrast, when groups

---

[3] Empirically we find that all initiative campaigns and nearly all referendum campaigns expend some resources on advertising. As I show in chapter 6, the amount of these expenditures varies dramatically across campaigns.

[4] Another advantage that groups seeking to preserve the status quo enjoy is that they must create doubt about only one or a few aspects of a new policy, whereas groups seeking to change the status quo must sell all or most aspects of the new policy.

try to mobilize a statewide electoral majority with strictly monetary resources, they may end up with limited monetary resources left to purchase critical campaign advertisements.

The second reason that monetary resources are not sufficient for mobilizing an electoral majority has to do with how voters process campaign information. When voters choose between direct legislation alternatives, they rely on the cues provided by groups and individuals that support and oppose the measure (Lupia 1994; Gerber and Lupia 1998). Observing the expenditure of personnel resources may convey to voters that people like them support the measure. Observing the expenditure of vast monetary resources, by contrast, may in fact turn voters away from the group's position if voters interpret those expenditures as indicating that narrow, wealthy economic interests, and not people like them, support the issue. Voters may interpret monetary expenditures in this way even if many voters also support the measure. In other words, the problem is with the perception of the group making monetary expenditures rather than with the reality of that group's interests. When groups are known to have interests that conflict with those of many voters, it may be even more difficult for these groups to use their monetary resources to overcome the impression that they fail to reflect the voters' interests.

Thus, to overcome the campaign-stage hurdles associated with direct preserving, indirect modifying, and indirect preserving influence, groups may expend either monetary or personnel resources. To overcome the campaign-stage hurdles associated with direct modifying strategies, groups must expend both monetary and personnel resources.

Postelection Stage

In the postelection stage, when groups propose initiatives or popular referendums, they must be able to defend their measures from legislative amendments or legal challenges. When they pose a legal challenge, groups must be able to organize the challenge. Orchestrating or defending against legislative amendments requires the same sorts of resources that any legislative strategy requires. In particular, groups require monetary resources in the form of campaign contributions to gain access to key legislative decision makers or personnel resources in the form of experts who can, through their testimony and lobbying, affect the content of legislation.[5] Orchestrating or defending against legal challenges also requires substantial resources. Groups must be able to draw on experts from within their group or hire experts to litigate the case. They also require monetary resources to fund their challenge or defense.

---

[5] Alternatively, groups can expend monetary resources to hire experts from outside the group.

Summary

Four aspects of table 4.1 warrant further attention. First, some specific direct legislation hurdles can be overcome with only one type of resource. For example, purchasing airtime for campaign ads requires cash. Only groups who have monetary resources can overcome this hurdle. By contrast, other hurdles, such as collecting signatures, can be overcome with either monetary or personnel resources. Groups with sufficient monetary resources can pay professional signature gatherers, and groups with sufficient personnel resources can call on volunteers to collect signatures. Note, however, that when monetary and personnel resources are substitutable for overcoming a particular hurdle, one resource may be more efficient than another. For example, it may be very expensive to buy certain types of expertise, whereas groups that have in-house experts can mobilize those resources at relatively low cost.

Second, even though groups can overcome the hurdles at the drafting, qualifying, and postelection stages with either monetary or personnel resources, they must possess both monetary and personnel resources to overcome campaign-stage hurdles associated with direct modifying influence. This means that groups that have difficulty mobilizing one resource or the other may be limited in their ability to achieve direct modifying influence and therefore restricted to other forms of influence.

Third, it is helpful to recall that the height of any particular hurdle can vary across elections, although some are relatively constant. For example, all groups that wish to qualify an initiative in a given state must obtain a fixed number of signatures. Although groups with fewer resources may find it more difficult to clear this hurdle, its height is exogenous and is the same for all groups.

The height of other hurdles varies across situations. For example, all groups must expend some resources to mobilize votes, but the quality and quantity of those efforts depend on the activities of other groups and the behavior of the voters themselves. When the other side runs a vigorous opposition campaign, groups must expend resources to counter the opposition's claims. This means that the campaign-stage hurdle is higher when there is competition from other groups. Similarly, when voters are strongly predisposed against an initiative measure, groups must make efforts to try to change their positions, thereby raising the hurdle at the campaign stage.

Finally, a group's goals will affect the height of the hurdles it faces. If groups want to pass a new law, they must run a victorious campaign. If, instead, groups merely seek to send a message to the legislature, it may be sufficient to receive less than a majority of the vote. Hence, groups who seek to influence policy by signaling the legislature may face lower hurdles than those who seek to influence policy by passing a new law by initiative.

Membership Characteristics

Just as a particular firm will find it easier to mobilize one type of resource (i.e., labor or capital), a particular interest group will also find it easier to mobilize one type of resource (i.e., personnel or monetary). In other words, groups have comparative advantages at mobilizing different types of resources. Thus, capital-intensive firms may be able to enhance their labor supply, but they may be able to do so only at very high cost. Likewise, although groups with a comparative advantage at raising monetary resources may also be able to mobilize personnel resources, doing so may be very costly. I argue that a group's comparative advantage at mobilizing monetary or personnel resources derives largely from its internal characteristics, particularly its membership composition.

Membership composition determines the nature of a group's collective action problem. All groups in the direct legislation process face two types of collective action problems. First, interest groups face an "internal" collective action problem that they must overcome in order to extract resources from their members or other sources.[6] Because the public policies that interest groups pursue tend to be nonexcludable collective goods, potential beneficiaries of a policy have an incentive to free ride off the efforts of those that join the group and contribute resources.[7] As Olson (1965, p. 28) showed, individuals acting in their personal economic self-interest will contribute suboptimal levels of resources toward the provision of a collective good. This means that voluntary associations such as interest groups must find ways to mobilize support because personal self-interest may not lead individuals to contribute sufficient resources.

Groups also face an "external" collective action problem. Because most public policies provide benefits to members of many different organizations, groups involved in direct legislation nearly always act in coalitions with other groups. Typically the members of one group cannot be excluded from receiving the policy benefits that result from another group's use of direct legislation. Therefore, any one group has an incentive to free ride off the efforts of other groups involved in the direct legislation process.

A group's ability to overcome these collective action problems derives largely from characteristics of its membership base.[8] A major distinction exists

[6] Walker (1991) stressed the importance of nonmembers such as government agencies, foundations, and wealthy citizens.

[7] Examples of nonexcludable collective goods include clean-air regulations that benefit everyone who breathes the cleaner air, regardless of whether they contribute to obtaining the regulations. Other public policies such as economic regulation also have many characteristics of nonexcludable collective goods.

[8] Olson (1965) argued that a group's size is a major determinant of its ability to mobilize members. He noted that the characteristics of individual members also matter in large groups with the most severe collective action problems.

between interest groups whose members are individual citizens and those whose members are representatives of corporations or other existing organizations. Borrowing Walker's terms, I describe these two types of members as *autonomous individuals* and *organizational representatives*, respectively.[9] Autonomous individuals join interest groups to represent themselves. Organizational representatives join interest groups to represent other organizations, typically their employers. Groups with each type of membership are able to mobilize different resources. A continuum underlies the range between groups composed exclusively of autonomous individuals and those composed entirely of organizational representatives. For illustrative purposes, I first consider the pure cases. I later consider the interim or mixed cases.

Individual Members

Interest groups whose members are autonomous individuals face a severe collective action problem. Potential members pay dues or make contributions from their own personal resources. The opportunity costs of such expenditures are acute. For many people, paying dues to a publicly minded interest group is not feasible because it means forgoing necessities. For others, paying dues to an interest group means a trade-off between membership and other expenditures. Unless individual members are extremely wealthy, the source of power for such groups is their large numbers. Even though large size allows groups to ask less of individual members, it further exacerbates the costs of collective action (Olson 1965). Offsetting this collective action problem is the fact that interest groups composed primarily of individual members are often involved in social and moral issues such as abortion, gay rights, gun control, and the death penalty. Members often feel very intensely about these issues and may join groups, despite the apparent economic irrationality of doing so, to receive the psychic or purposive benefits associated with involvement in these issues (Salisbury 1969).

All else constant, groups that are composed of autonomous individuals are expected to mobilize personnel resources more easily than monetary resources. Groups can mobilize personnel resources when individuals are willing and able to devote their time and energy to advocating the group's agenda. Individuals may do so when they feel strongly about the group's political agenda, such as when the group deals with moral or social issues. Individuals may also be willing to devote their time and energy to the group's agenda when they receive selective incentives (i.e., benefits that can be withheld from nonparticipants) for their participation.

---

[9] Walker (1991) focused primarily on how membership type affects a group's strategies for member recruitment and retention. I focus instead on how membership composition affects the types of resources a group can raise.

Organizational Members

Interest groups whose members are organizational representatives face different problems in extracting and dedicating resources. Individual members rarely pay their own dues. Instead, dues are paid by the organizations they represent. In addition, members participate in interest group activities on company time or as part of their work responsibilities. Thus, because less of their personal time, effort, and resources are required, the direct, personal opportunity costs of membership to the organizational representative are not as severe as when autonomous individuals contribute to a group's cause.

All else constant, groups whose members are primarily organizational representatives are expected to have a comparative advantage at mobilizing monetary resources. Because organizational representatives rely on their companies to pay their dues, the members of these groups face a less severe collective action problem because they need not absorb the personal opportunity costs of their contributions. Thus, groups composed of organizational representatives can extract monetary resources from their members more easily than groups composed of autonomous individuals. Furthermore, most organizations have resource bases that are substantially greater than those enjoyed by single individuals; in other words, they have deep pockets. Hence, interest groups whose members are primarily organizational representatives find that their potential members have abundant monetary resources and that these resources are easier to extract.

Importance of Membership Characteristics

The distinction between groups whose members are organizational representatives and those whose are autonomous individuals closely parallels Walker's (1991) typology of occupational versus citizen groups. In their chapter on "The Ecology of Interest Groups in America," King and Walker (1991) drew a primary distinction between whether or not the group places restrictions on its membership. Occupational groups "require members to possess certain professional or occupational credentials," whereas citizen groups "are open to all citizens regardless of their qualifications" (p. 58). King and Walker then further subdivided occupational interest groups by those whose members are drawn primarily from the profit sector (e.g., Mortgage Bankers Association, Aerospace Industries), the nonprofit sector (e.g., Association of American Medical Colleges, National Association of Student Financial Aid Administrators), and the mixed sector (e.g., Society of American Foresters, American Hospital Association). This further subdivision is motivated by King and Walker's interest in analyzing the sources of financial support to groups, which varies in important ways from sector to sector.[10]

Although King and Walker's ultimate four-sector categorization is appropriate for answering questions about a group's sources of support, it is less well suited to understanding the types of resources that groups are able to mobilize, the strategies that they are likely to choose, and the forms of influence that they are able to achieve. To answer these questions, which is the purpose of my categorization, the important distinction concerns members' motivations for joining and whether these motivations are occupational. These motivations, in turn, underlie a group's ability to solve collective action problems and thereby mobilize resources. Undoubtedly, member motivations may closely parallel a group's membership restrictions: Organizational representatives may be more likely to join groups that restrict membership to individuals possessing certain professional or occupational credentials; autonomous individuals may be more likely to join groups that are open to all members regardless of their qualifications. Likewise, groups with professional or occupational restrictions may have predominantly organizational representatives as members, whereas groups with no such restrictions may attract predominantly autonomous individuals. I do not expect this correlation to be perfect, however. Most important, groups that lack membership restrictions may have either organizational representatives or autonomous individuals as members. Therefore, I focus on membership composition rather than group requirements in order to emphasize the importance of member motivations and consequently the group's ability to overcome collective action problems.

Furthermore, my distinction between groups whose members are primarily organizational representatives and groups whose members are primarily autonomous individuals reflects my substantive motivation to assess the populist paradox. As I will discuss in more detail below, the economic interest groups that so concerned both the Populist and Progressive reformers and the modern-day critics of the direct legislation process are precisely those groups whose members are predominantly organizational representatives. The broad-based citizen groups whose interests the Populists, Progressives, and modern-day reformers wished to promote are precisely those groups whose members are autonomous individuals. Therefore, my distinction between groups based on their membership composition is directed at addressing both the theoretical and empirical questions that motivate this study.[11]

---

[10] Note that King and Walker (1991) excluded trade unions from their analysis because membership in them is typically not voluntary. However, because unions are important actors in the direct legislation process, I include them as a separate category in my analysis.

[11] Note that, although my primary distinction among groups is based on membership composition, this distinction also implies other systematic differences across categories. First, groups with different membership bases may pursue different issues. Second, groups with different membership bases may be characterized by different internal organizational structures. In terms of resource mobilization and choice of strategy, however, a group's membership composition and not its substantive interests or internal organization is primary.

TABLE 4.2
Groups and Resource Comparative Advantages

Group Type	Membership Composition	Resource Advantage
Business	Organizational representative	Monetary
Economic interest group	Organizational representative	Monetary
Professional interest group	Organizational representative or autonomous individual	Monetary or personnel
Trade union	Autonomous individual	Personnel
Citizen interest group	Autonomous individual	Personnel

Classifying Groups and Their Resources

Groups can be classified according to their membership characteristics. I argue that these characteristics translate into comparative advantages at raising monetary and personnel resources. These resources can in turn be used to overcome hurdles and ultimately influence policy. Table 4.2 reports the relationship between the major types of direct legislation users, their membership characteristics, and their comparative resource advantages.

The primary distinction in table 4.2 is between economic interest groups and citizen interest groups. These groups represent the (near) endpoints on the continuum between groups whose members are strictly organizational representatives and groups whose members are strictly autonomous individuals.[12] Economic interest groups include trade associations such as the California Beer and Wine Wholesalers Association, the Air Transport Association of America, the Missouri Forest Products Association, and the Washington Software Association. Each of these groups was an active participant in state politics in one or more states in the late 1980s or early 1990s. Members of these economic interest groups join as representatives of their employers or businesses (if self-employed). These groups may restrict their memberships to organizational representatives with professional or occupational credentials; more important, however, there is little incentive for autonomous individuals who are not employed within the industry to join these groups.

Citizen interest groups include organizations whose members join for nonoccupational reasons. These include partisan political organizations such as political parties and groups like the Lincoln Club of Orange County. They include nonpartisan political organizations such as the League of Women Voters. They also include noneconomic organizations such as the National Rifle Association, the Sierra Club, and the American Civil Liberties Union, as

---

[12] In my subsequent analysis, I argue that single businesses and corporations in fact define the endpoint of groups made up of only organization representatives. Economic interest groups may have some autonomous individuals as members.

well as nonoccupational groups that are concerned with economic issues such as the California Taxpayers Association.[13]

Because economic groups and citizen groups have different membership characteristics, I expect them to have different resource bases. Economic groups have primarily organizational representatives as members, which results in a comparative advantage in amassing monetary resources. By contrast, citizen groups have autonomous individuals as members, which gives them a comparative advantage in mobilizing personnel resources but may prevent them from extracting monetary resources.

In addition to citizen and economic interest groups, other types of interest groups use the direct legislation process as well. Like economic and citizen groups, these other groups can be classified according to their membership characteristics. I argue that their membership characteristics, like those of economic and citizen groups, result in comparative advantages at mobilizing monetary and personnel resources.

A third type of group that uses direct legislation is a single business or corporation. For example, in the 1994 general election, businesses as diverse as the Container Supply Company, GE Financial Services, Southern Pacific Transportation Co., Atlantic Richfield Co., Chevron Corporation, Union Oil Company of CA, PacifiCare of California, and Philip Morris USA contributed $10,000 or more to California ballot measure campaigns (California Secretary of State 1994). Thousands of businesses made smaller contributions. For these and other corporations, political decisions are business decisions. "Membership" in a corporation differs from membership in other interest groups because individuals do not join voluntarily but rather become part of the corporation as a condition of their employment. Thus, members are organizational representatives in the strictest sense. I therefore expect monetary resources to dominate their resource base.

A fourth type of group that uses the direct legislation process is a professional interest group. These groups include professionals such as doctors, lawyers, and architects whose personal interests and resources are indistinguishable from those of their profession. In other words, a professional's personal wealth is a direct function of his or her business's wealth; the more money the business makes, the more the individual doctor or lawyer makes.[14] Examples of politically active professional interest groups include the California Trial Lawyers Association and the California Optometric Association.[15] Like members of economic interest groups or corporations, professionals often make

---

[13] These examples of citizen interest groups are also drawn from the population of groups that were active in state politics in one or more states (i.e., they contributed monetary resources) between 1988 and 1992.

[14] The relationship between the individual and his or her profession becomes more complicated when the professional is a member of a group or partnership. Nonetheless, the linkage is much closer than in regular employment-based corporations.

[15] Note that I consider individual lawyers, doctors, and other professionals as businesses and their associations as professional interest groups.

political contributions out of their professional resources. However, unlike members of economic interest groups and corporations who are paid wages or salaries, professionals' expenditures directly affect their personal resources.[16] In this sense, membership composition falls somewhere between economic groups with their organizational representatives and citizen groups with their autonomous individual members.

Because the ability to allocate dues as professional expenses offsets some of the personal costs of a contribution, I expect professional interest groups to mobilize monetary resources more effectively than groups whose members are strictly autonomous individuals. However, I expect the ability of professional interest groups to extract these resources to be lower than for economic interest groups and corporations that have strictly organizational members. Because their members may have more of a personal stake in the group's activities, then I expect professional interest groups to generate a greater potential source of personnel resources than businesses of economic groups

A fifth type of group that uses the direct legislation process is an occupational association or trade union. Members join trade unions because of their occupation or employment. However, members are not official representatives of their employer but autonomous individuals who pay their own dues. I therefore expect monetary resources to be scarce. Because of their large memberships, unions have a comparative advantage at raising personnel resources. Indeed, I expect unions to possess more personnel resources than either strictly economic or professional interest groups.

To summarize, because their memberships comprise primarily organizational representatives, I expect businesses and corporations, like economic interest groups, to have a comparative advantage at mobilizing monetary resources. Because their memberships comprise primarily autonomous individuals, I expect trade unions, like citizen interest groups, to have a comparative advantage at mobilizing personnel resources. By contrast, I expect professional interest groups, which reflect a hybrid between organizational representatives and autonomous individuals, to mobilize a mix of monetary and personnel resources.

Hypotheses about Motivations and Forms of Influence

Groups select forms of influence that correspond to the types of resources they are able to mobilize. Based on my prior discussions of the institutional and behavioral hurdles associated with each form of influence and the resources different types of groups can amass, I now generate a set of empirically testable hypotheses.

---

[16] Many corporations tie compensation to performance, especially for managers. In such cases, expenditures on political activities may reduce an individual's personal resources. These political expenditures only indirectly affect an individual's personal resources, however.

Direct Modifying Influence

Groups that have substantial personnel resources plus a large stock of monetary resources will be able to overcome high campaign-stage hurdles. These groups may be able to achieve direct modifying influence. As I discussed earlier in this chapter, running a successful direct legislation campaign requires expending substantial sums of money to purchase campaign advertisements. Monetary resources, however, are not sufficient. Groups also require personnel resources to mobilize diverse interests, build networks with other groups, fundraise, coordinate campaign-related activities, signal grassroots support, and otherwise generate an electoral majority.

Few groups can mobilize both monetary and personnel resources. As discussed earlier in this chapter, however, citizen groups have the internal characteristics that provide them with a substantial advantage at mobilizing personnel resources. Some citizen groups may also be able to raise monetary resources. Groups that are able to raise both types of resources may then be able to pursue direct modifying influence. Thus, I hypothesize that *citizen groups will pursue direct modifying influence more often than they will pursue direct preserving influence.* Because citizen groups are better able to mobilize personnel resources than are economic groups, I also hypothesize that *citizen groups will pursue direct modifying influence relatively more often than will economic groups.*[17] Note that the point here is not that citizen groups prefer strategies with high campaign-stage hurdles per se. Rather, there may be extra policy benefits in terms of controlling the policy agenda associated with pursuing direct modifying influence. Their personnel resources, when combined with sufficient monetary resources, allow some citizen groups to overcome high campaign-stage hurdles in order to receive these high policy benefits.

Direct Preserving Influence

Because generating an electoral majority in favor of a new policy requires both monetary and personnel resources, groups that have a comparative advantage at raising monetary resources and have difficulty mobilizing personnel resources will have difficulty achieving victory at the ballot box. Consequently,

---

[17] I modify this hypothesis with the term "relatively" to account for the possibility that economic (citizen) groups may be more active in the direct legislation process overall and so may engage in both direct modifying and direct preserving (and perhaps other) forms of influence more often than do citizen (economic) groups. This modified hypothesis states that I expect the use of direct modifying strategies, as a share of all direct legislation activities, to be greater for citizen groups.

these groups will have trouble overcoming high campaign-stage hurdles. Instead of pursuing direct modifying influence, groups with a comparative advantage at mobilizing monetary resources will have an incentive to seek status quo preserving influence or indirect influence (either preserving or modifying) because they entail lower campaign-stage hurdles. Economic groups have a comparative advantage at mobilizing monetary resources. Thus, I hypothesize that *economic groups will more often pursue direct preserving influence than direct modifying influence.* I also hypothesize that *economic groups will pursue direct preserving influence relatively more often than will citizen groups.*[18]

Indirect Influence

Indirect influence involves pressuring the legislature to pass or block legislation. As discussed in chapter 2, interest groups can use direct legislation to pressure the legislature in at least two ways: by threatening to pass adverse initiatives and by signaling the interest group's position on a policy. Which groups can threaten to pass adverse initiatives? Economic interest groups have an advantage in mobilizing the monetary resources required to run an initiative campaign. These resources, however, are not sufficient to pass new initiatives: if the initiatives that economic groups propose cannot win, then their threats to pass initiatives are not credible. Citizen groups face greater difficulty mobilizing monetary resources but typically have more personnel resources. When they can mobilize sufficient monetary and personnel resources to run an effective campaign, the measures they support have a higher probability of passing. As a result, their threats to pass initiatives that the legislature opposes may be more credible. Thus, I hypothesize that *citizen groups will more often pursue indirect influence by threatening to pass adverse initiatives than will economic groups.*

What types of groups are best able to use direct legislation to signal their position on an issue? To signal their preferences, interest groups expend either monetary or personnel resources. When groups expend monetary resources to signal their position, the important factor is how much they spend. This spending signals how much the measure means to the group. The groups most likely to use this strategy are economic interest groups. Their monetary resources allow economic groups to purchase expensive campaign ads to attract the electorate's, and hence legislators', attention. Economic groups may also be less constrained by their members to pursue popular issues and may instead pursue their most preferred policy without regard to whether the measure will actually pass. On issues in which an interest group's policy preferences

---

[18] I use the term "relatively more often" in the same sense as above.

coincide with those of a substantial number of legislators, I therefore hypothe-size that *economic groups will more often expend monetary resources to sig-nal their support of, or opposition to, an issue to the legislature than will citizen groups.*

When groups expend personnel resources to signal their position, the im-portant factor is how many voters they can mobilize. In an attempt to mo-bilize voters, campaign spending per se is less important. Rather, it is more important for the group to engage in grassroots and campaign activities to mobilize supporters, volunteers, and ultimately votes. It may also be advan-tageous for the group to draft and qualify the measure itself as a further in-dicator of grassroots support. These activities require a mix of personnel re-sources to mobilize grassroots support and monetary resources to run an effective campaign. As discussed earlier in this chapter, the groups most likely to possess a combination of personnel and monetary resources are citi-zen interest groups. Thus, I hypothesize that *citizen groups will more often expend personnel resources to signal voter support than will economic groups.*

My hypotheses about direct forms of influence contain both intra- and inter-group hypotheses. I predict both that citizen groups will pursue some forms of influence (i.e., direct modifying) more often than others (i.e., direct preserv-ing) and that citizen groups will pursue direct modifying influence more often than will economic groups. Similarly, I produce both intra- and intergroup hypotheses for the greater use of direct preserving influence by economic groups. By contrast, I produce only intergroup hypotheses about the use of the various forms of indirect influence. On the basis of the theory, it is impossible to predict whether, for example, citizen groups will more often pursue indirect influence by threatening to pass adverse initiatives or by expending personnel resources to signal their preferences. In other words, our inferences are limited to comparisons between the expected use of these strategies by groups with different resource advantages. Understanding the relative importance of these several forms of indirect influence by a given group type must come, instead, from our empirical analysis.

To summarize, I hypothesize that economic interest groups and other groups with primarily monetary resources will pursue direct preserving influ-ence or indirect forms of influence that involve low campaign-stage hurdles. Citizen interest groups and other groups with high levels of personnel re-sources will pursue direct modifying influence. In terms of the relative influ-ence of economic and citizen interest groups, these hypotheses make it clear that we expect each group to have different types of influence. We expect the influence of citizen interest groups to be directed toward modifying the status quo. By contrast, we expect economic interest groups to direct their influence toward preserving the status quo or pressuring other actors.

Summary

This chapter explores the relationship between a group's membership characteristics and its resource base. By categorizing groups according to their internal characteristics and by considering how these characteristics translate into advantages at mobilizing certain types of resources, I posit differences in the mix of resources that different kinds of groups possess. I argue that groups whose members are primarily organizational representatives can raise monetary resources at relatively low cost, whereas groups whose members are primarily autonomous individuals can more easily mobilize personnel resources.

Having established the relationship between a group's membership characteristics and its resource base, I generated a set of hypotheses about the relationship between a group's resource base, the forms of influence that it will pursue, and the particular strategies that it will adopt. I argue that groups choose strategies requiring the resources that reflect their comparative advantage. From the perspective of the populist paradox, the most important implication of these hypotheses is that economic interest groups are quite limited in the ways that they can use direct legislation to influence policy.

The remainder of this book is devoted to testing the hypotheses about interest group strategies and influence. In the next chapter, I test hypotheses about interest group motivations and activities by analyzing campaign contribution activities and a survey of groups that use the direct legislation process. I then use these analyses to clarify the policy consequences of lawmaking by direct legislation. In the concluding chapter, I explain how differences in interest group influence translate into who wins and who loses in the political process.

5

Motivations and Strategies

CHAPTERS 1 THROUGH 4 develop a theory of interest group choice. The theory is based on the notion that groups pursue forms of influence and political strategies that involve low costs, relative to the expected benefits of pursuing the strategies. These costs are a function of the institutional and behavioral hurdles associated with each strategy and the types of resources groups are able to mobilize. Because economic interest groups and citizen interest groups have different comparative advantages at mobilizing resources, I expect them to use the direct legislation process in different ways. I hypothesize that citizen interest groups will try to influence policy directly because they can use their resources to mobilize electoral support. I hypothesize that economic interest groups, by contrast, will pursue forms of influence that require less electoral support, such as blocking laws they oppose or pressuring the legislature.

In this chapter, I present the first empirical tests of my hypotheses. I test these hypotheses by answering two questions. First, how do groups describe their motivations for using direct legislation and their predominant direct legislation activities? Second, how do groups actually use the process?

Methodology

The data for my empirical tests come from two sources. The first data source is a survey of interest groups in four states that allow direct legislation. The data from this survey allow me to answer the first question: What do groups say they do?

In the spring of 1996, I conducted the survey in conjunction with the Faculty Mentor Program at the University of California, San Diego.[1] I mailed the survey to six hundred interest groups, approximately half of whom I identified as direct legislation users and half of whom I identified as nonusers.[2] In the cover letter, I explained the purpose of the survey and ensured the confidentiality of responses. In the survey itself, I asked groups about their use of direct legislation and other political activities during the last five years. For groups that reported some use of direct legislation, I then asked what they hoped to accom-

---

[1] I thank Christopher DenHartog, Michael Holman, Daniel Murdock, Neelima Shah, Gina Simas, and Amanda Smith for their involvement in writing and administering the survey.

[2] I provide details on how I identified users and nonusers below.

plish and why they chose direct legislation. For groups that reported not using direct legislation in the last five years, I asked why they chose not to use direct legislation. For both users and nonusers, I also asked about the group's other political activities and about organizational features of the group such as type, membership size and composition, source of funds, and policy areas. I received 156 of the 600 surveys completed, resulting in a response rate of about 26 percent. A copy of the survey is included in Appendix B.

The interest groups in my survey are sampled from four states: California, Oregon, Idaho, and Nebraska. These states represent a subset of the sample of states used in the analysis of campaign finance activity that I describe later in this chapter. The four states, although not a random sample of direct legislation states, reflect a good deal of diversity in their patterns of use of the direct legislation process. Specifically, California and Oregon are high-use states, Nebraska is a moderate-use state, and Idaho is a low-use state. The states also differ in terms of institutional hurdles (especially signature requirements, preelection review, and postelection amendability) and behavioral hurdles (i.e., the cost of running a winning direct legislation campaign).

The sample of groups that used direct legislation is drawn from the population of interest groups in the four states that made financial contributions to direct legislation campaigns between 1988 and 1992.[3] To identify these direct legislation users, I obtained reports of contributions to every committee formed to support or oppose direct legislation propositions in each state. In all of the states included in my sample, individuals, businesses, and interest groups make contributions to ballot measure committees, who then channel those contributions to the campaigns. These committees are then responsible for disclosing the sources of the contributions. Disclosure reports detail the sources of the original contributions to the ballot measure committees. In sum, these reports disclose the contributions of thousands of contributors to 129 separate ballot measures. All of the states in my sample report the contributor's name and the amount of the contribution above some amount in the disclosure reports.[4] Some states also report the contributor's occupation, type, and/or address.

The sample of groups that did not use direct legislation is drawn from the population of interest groups in the four states that contributed to statewide candidate (typically governor) campaigns between 1988 and 1992. To identify these nonusers, I obtained the contribution reports for the office(s) in question.[5]

---

[3] In 1992, California changed its reporting requirements, requiring disclosure of contributions over $10,000 only; therefore, California data are from 1988 and 1990 only.

[4] This amount ranges between $100 and $250.

[5] The populations of users and nonusers are not mutually exclusive. Therefore, some of the groups in the subsample of contributors to statewide candidate campaigns may also include contributors to direct legislation campaigns, and vice versa. In the surveys, I ask the groups to identify

TABLE 5.1
Number of Survey Respondents

	Direct Legislation		
Group Type	User	Nonuser	Total
Business	18	13	31
Economic + Professional	43	36	79
Occupational	13	3	16
Citizen	18	12	30
Total	92	64	156

Based on the contributors' names, reported types or occupations, and secondary sources, a team of graduate students and myself coded each contribution according to the contributor's type (i.e., business, economic interest group, professional interest group, occupational interest group, citizen interest group, individual or candidate).[6] From the coded contribution reports, I then randomly selected subsamples from five of the group types from each state. The sample of users therefore includes businesses, economic interest groups, professional interest groups, occupational interest groups, and citizen interest groups from the four states. The sample of nonusers also includes businesses, economic interest groups, professional interest groups, occupational interest groups, and citizen interest groups from the four states.

Table 5.1 reports the number of responses by group type for users and nonusers. Given the small number of completed responses, I am limited in the comparisons I will be able to make in several ways. First, because there are few observations from each state and because my hypotheses say little about differences in interest group behavior across states, I combine my observations from

---

themselves as direct legislation users or nonusers and rely on those self-reports in the analysis below.

[6] In some ways, the actual data are insufficient to provide a complete categorization of groups. Most important, even with our careful coding procedures and use of secondary sources, I recognize that it is impossible to infer accurately all contributors' constituency bases from the limited available information. In some cases, differences among occupational, professional, and economic interest groups are quite subtle, and such distinctions require judgment calls. In other cases, businesses or economic groups may adopt names such as "Californians against Unfair Rate Increases" or "Consumers for Low Insurance Rates." Despite the grassroots images their names suggest, these committees received virtually all of their funding ($14 million and $5 million, respectively) in 1988 from the insurance industry (California Fair Political Practices Commission 1988b).

In the analysis of the survey responses, I rely on groups' self-identification. Therefore, the coding is only important insofar as it affected my selection of the original sample of groups to be included in the survey. In the analysis of campaign contribution activity below, coding issues are more important. To address some of these concerns, I consider the percentage of contributions from each of the seven types of contributors, and I combine some of the categories. Although I am more confident in the combined comparison, because it requires fewer distinctions between the contributors, I believe important information can also be garnered from the comparison of each group type as well.

the four states. This initial grouping results in eight basic categories.[7] Second, because there are still few observations in some of the resulting categories, I further combine responses from businesses, economic groups, and professional groups that used direct legislation; citizen group and occupational group users; businesses, economic group, and professional group nonusers; and citizen group and occupational group nonusers. The resulting data allow me to test hypotheses about differences in motivations and activities both within and among these group categorizations.

As a tool for studying interest group activities and motivations, the surveys have the advantage of asking groups directly how and why they used the political process. Like all surveys, however, they also carry the possibility of response bias. In these particular surveys, the most likely sources of response bias are a lack of information on the part of the individual completing the survey, reporting biases (especially post hoc justifications for the group's activities), and concerns about confidentiality. To minimize the potential for such bias, I worded the questions as unambiguously as possible, extensively pretested the survey instrument, and assured the groups that the surveys were for noncommercial, academic purposes only.

The second data source allows me to answer somewhat different questions about interest group motivations and strategies. My second method involves analyzing data on what interest groups actually do. These data are campaign finance records from the four states in the survey plus Maine, Michigan, Missouri, and Washington. As described above, the campaign finance reports disclose each individual contribution from regular citizens, businesses, candidates, or organized interest groups to each committee formed to support or oppose each ballot proposition. I coded the campaign finance data as described above for all initiatives and referendums qualified for the 1988–1992 ballots in the eight states.[8] In total, we were able to code over 98 percent of all contributions to the 161 ballot measures included in the study.[9]

The main reason for including these eight states in the sample is that these states (1) required contributors to statewide initiative and referendum campaigns to report their financial activities, and (2) made such information publicly available. In addition, even though they do not represent a random sample of direct legislation states, the eight states in my sample, like the four states in my survey sample, reflect a wide range of different experiences with direct

---

[7] These eight categories correspond to the four categories on the surveys (i.e., business, economic/professional, union, and citizen) into which groups were asked to self-identify as users or nonusers. Although I differentiate between economic and professional interest groups in my theory, I was concerned that such distinctions would be lost on my survey respondents, and I therefore combined those two categories. To the extent that there are important differences between economic and professional interest groups, combining them into one category will attenuate these differences in my analyses.

[8] The California data include only 1988 and 1990.

[9] The 161 measures include 81 from California, 3 from Idaho, 5 from Maine, 7 from Michigan, 16 from Missouri, 15 from Nebraska, 24 from Oregon, and 10 from Washington.

legislation. Some of the states in the sample have a long Progressive history, but others do not. For many years, Oregon was the most frequent user of direct legislation (Dubois and Feeney 1992). In recent years, however, California has surpassed Oregon. Several of the states in the sample have moderate use of direct legislation (Michigan, Missouri, and Nebraska), whereas others use it only rarely (Idaho, and Maine). The states also differ on several institutional and behavioral variables such as signature requirement, amendment provisions, and campaign costs.

The primary advantage of using campaign finance data to test hypotheses about interest group activities and motivations is that the data describe what groups actually did rather than what they say they did. The primary disadvantage is that the inferences one can draw, especially about a group's motivations, are indirect. In other words, it may be difficult to infer a group's motivation for making a particular contribution because that behavior may be consistent with several motivations (e.g., with achieving either direct or indirect influence). The second disadvantage is that the campaign finance data reflect only a subset of interest group activities in the direct legislation process, that is, activities that involve financial contributions to direct legislation campaign committees. In testing intragroup hypotheses, I will therefore be restricted to those that deal with activities involving the use of monetary resources.

Overall, the two data sets complement each other in several ways. The surveys provide a large amount of information about a small number of groups, and the campaign finance data provide more limited information about a much larger sample of groups. The surveys provide direct evidence of interest group motivations and activities but are subject to respondent error and response bias. The campaign finance data provide only indirect evidence of interest group motivations but are free from the errors that plague surveys. Because of these characteristics, the surveys allow me to make both within-group comparisons about the motivations and activities of each group type and some across-group comparisons. The campaign finance data allow me to make across-group comparisons about the differences in some motivations and activities of different groups but only limited within-group comparisons. Because of these limitations in each data set and the complementarity between the two data sets, the greatest power of these empirical analyses will thus lie not in the results of a single test but rather in the broad patterns of behavior that emerge from both data sets.

What Do Groups Say They Do?

I first analyze data from my survey of interest groups to test hypotheses about interest group motivations and activities. The data allow me to answer questions about what forms of influence different types of groups report they were trying to achieve and what activities they undertook to achieve that influence.

Interest Group Motivations

I hypothesize that, because of their comparative advantages at mobilizing personnel resources, citizen groups will try to achieve direct modifying influence. By contrast, I hypothesize that, because they are better able to mobilize monetary resources, economic groups will try to achieve forms of influence, such as pressuring the legislature, that require monetary resources.

To test these hypotheses, I asked a set of questions regarding group motivations for using direct legislation. Among these questions, I asked groups the importance of the following ten objectives in their organization's decision to use direct legislation.

MOTIVATIONS FOR USING DIRECT LEGISLATION

- **A.** Passing desired legislation by initiative or referendum
- **B.** Sending a signal to the state legislature about popular support for an issue
- **C.** Pressuring the state legislature to place a new issue on its legislative agenda
- **D.** Pressuring the state legislature to pass desired legislation
- **E.** Drawing public attention to your organization
- **F.** Drawing public attention to your organization's political agenda
- **G.** Protecting legislation from amendments by the legislature
- **H.** Complying with constitutional requirements
- **I.** Responding to member demands for action
- **J.** Developing networks with other organizations
- **K.** Other

Motivations A through D relate directly to forms of influence described in the theory. Passing legislation by initiative (A) is a form of direct modifying influence. I therefore hypothesize that citizen interest groups will report passing legislation by initiative as a more important objective than the other motivations. Sending a signal (B) and pressuring the legislature (C and D) are forms of indirect influence that require monetary or personnel resources. I hypothesize that economic groups will report that sending a signal and pressuring the legislature (B, C, and D) are more important motivations than passing new laws by initiative.[10] Drawing attention to the group (E) or the group's

---

[10] Unfortunately, I did not ask questions about blocking legislation in the surveys, and I am therefore limited in my ability to draw inferences about the pursuit of direct preserving influence

TABLE 5.2
Motivations for Using Direct Legislation, Mean Values, Raw Responses

Motivation	Economic Professional Business	Citizen Occupational	t	Pr > |t|
Pass initiatives	3.04	4.25	−3.27	.0016
	N = 53	N = 24		
Signal support to legislature	3.75	4.28	−1.77	.0798
	N = 52	N = 25		
Set legislative agenda	3.50	3.92	−1.31	.1953
	N = 52	N = 25		
Pressure legislature to pass laws	3.74	4.08	−1.07	.2891
	N = 53	N = 25		
Draw attention to group	2.38	3.60	−3.76	.0003
	N = 50	N = 25		
Draw attention to agenda	2.31	3.48	−3.57	.0006
	N = 49	N = 25		
Protect from amendments	3.39	4.24	−2.52	.0140
	N = 51	N = 25		
Constitutional requirements	2.90	3.50	−1.60	.1150
	N = 48	N = 24		
Respond to members	3.79	4.12	−1.08	.2848
	N = 53	N = 25		
Develop networks	3.65	4.13	−1.62	.1105
	N = 51	N = 24		

Source: Survey of interest groups: California, Idaho, Nebraska, Oregon (see App. B).

agenda (F), protecting legislation from amendments (G), complying with constitutional requirements (H), responding to member demands (I), and developing networks (J) are other possible motivations for using direct legislation that may require some mix of monetary and personnel resources. Although the theory does not explicitly address motivations E through J, they may be important factors in the decision by both economic and citizen groups to use direct legislation.

Table 5.2 reports the mean importance of each objective for direct legislation users that self-identified as economic groups, professional groups, and businesses and for those that self-identified as citizen and occupational groups. Responses range from 1 (not at all important) to 5 (very important). Higher values therefore reflect greater importance.

from this data source. However, I can use the analysis of the second data source, campaign disclosure reports, to gain insight into how and when groups pursue direct preserving influence.

Of the four motivations about which the theory makes direct predictions (A–D), patterns of responses from economic interest groups, professional groups, and businesses largely conform to our expectations. The second column in table 5.2 shows that economic groups, professional groups, and businesses (hereafter, economic interests) attribute high levels of importance to signaling and pressuring the legislature and much lower levels of importance to passing new laws by initiative. Economic interests also attribute high levels of importance to responding to member demands for action, building networks with other groups, and protecting legislation against amendments, and low levels of importance to drawing attention to their organization and their organization's agenda and complying with constitutional requirements. Overall economic interests attribute the greatest importance to responding to member demands, signaling and pressuring the legislature, and developing networks with other groups.

A different pattern emerges when we analyze the motivations for using direct legislation reported by citizen and occupational groups. The third column shows that citizen and occupational groups (hereafter, citizen interests) attribute a much greater level of importance to passing new laws by initiative. In fact, only sending a signal to the legislature is of greater importance, and only marginally so. Protecting legislation from amendments is their next most important motivation, presumably reflecting their inability to protect their interests directly through the legislative process. Other forms of indirect influence (pressuring the legislature to place a new issue on its agenda or to pass existing legislative proposals) are substantially less important.

These comparisons within group types provide strong preliminary evidence in support of my intragroup hypotheses. Some analysis also stands to be made between groups as well. The fourth and fifth columns of table 5.2 report the *t*-statistic and significance level, respectively, for a test of the difference between the mean values of the economic interests and of the citizen interests for each motivation. The *t*-test is identical to the *t*-statistic obtained by regressing each objective on a dummy variable scored one for economic groups, professional groups, and businesses, plus a constant. The null hypothesis is that the means are equal.

The *t*-test shows that economic and citizen interests differ significantly in the importance they attribute to passing laws by initiative. Citizen interests report an average importance of 4.25, whereas economic interests report an average importance of only 3.04. This difference is statistically significant at the .05 level. Citizen and economic interests also attribute significantly different levels of importance to drawing attention to their organization, drawing attention to their organization's agenda, and protecting legislation from amendments.

A glance at the raw data, however, suggests that using this *t*-test to conclude that citizen interests attribute significantly more importance to passing new

TABLE 5.3
Motivations for Using Direct Legislation, Mean Values, Transformed Responses,
$\delta = 1.402936$

Motivation	Economic Professional Business	Citizen Occupational	t	$Pr > \lvert t \rvert$
Pass initiatives	4.26	4.25	.02	.9810
	$N = 53$	$N = 24$		
Signal support to legislature	5.26	4.28	2.49	.0148
	$N = 52$	$N = 25$		
Set legislative agenda	4.91	3.92	2.33	.0225
	$N = 52$	$N = 25$		
Pressure legislature to pass laws	5.24	4.08	2.70	.0086
	$N = 53$	$N = 25$		
Draw attention to group	3.34	3.60	−.63	.5326
	$N = 50$	$N = 25$		
Draw attention to agenda	3.24	3.48	−.58	.5622
	$N = 49$	$N = 25$		
Protect from amendments	4.76	4.24	1.16	.2505
	$N = 51$	$N = 25$		
Constitutional requirements	4.06	3.50	1.14	.2585
	$N = 48$	$N = 24$		
Respond to members	5.32	4.12	3.00	.0037
	$N = 53$	$N = 25$		
Develop networks	5.12	4.13	2.50	.0146
	$N = 51$	$N = 24$		

Source: Survey of interest groups (App. B).

initiatives is premature. Comparing the mean importance of each motivation shows that citizen interests attribute more importance to *all* of the ten motivations, although only four of these differences are statistically significant. This pattern therefore indicates some evidence of response bias on the part of one or both types of groups (either citizen interests are systematically overreporting importance or economic interests are underreporting importance, or both).

To correct for potential response bias, I multiply the economic interests' responses by a factor of 1.402936, which is the ratio of the mean citizen interest importance averaged over all ten motivations to the mean economic interest importance.[11] These transformed responses are reported in table 5.3.

[11] Of course, transforming the economic interest responses by a different factor would result in different intergroup comparisons. Specifically, transforming the economic interest responses by a factor of 1.13 retains the statistical significance of the difference in mean importance of passing new laws by initiative. Although I could have used any arbitrary transformation, the one I report

The responses in table 5.3 show that once we account for response bias, economic interests no longer attribute less importance to passing new laws by initiative. They do, however, attribute significantly more importance to signaling and pressuring the legislature, responding to member demands, and developing networks with other groups.

I now consider what factors led direct legislation users to pursue their political interests via direct legislation rather than some other policy arena. The logic of the theory suggests that a group's decision to use direct legislation depends on its resources. I asked users how important each of the following was when their organization decided to use direct legislation.

IMPORTANCE FOR USING DIRECT LEGISLATION

A. Familiarity with the direct legislation process
B. High probability of qualifying an initiative
C. High probability of passing an initiative or referendum
D. Difficulty of using the legislative process (i.e., state legislature)
E. Previous experience with direct legislation
F. Availability of consultants
G. Support from members
H. Availability of resources
I. Availability of volunteers

The second and third columns of table 5.4 report the importance of each factor for economic interests and citizen interests respectively.

Economic interests attribute the most importance to member support, familiarity with the process, availability of resources, and previous experience with direct legislation. In other words, they emphasize the importance of internal factors or constraints that may affect their costs. Citizen interests attribute the most importance to familiarity with the process and previous experience, suggesting that many may find the prospect of running a statewide direct legislation campaign, especially for the first time, quite daunting. Citizen interests also attach high importance to the perceived probability of qualifying and passing an initiative. In other words, they emphasize external factors that may contribute to their success.

These data exhibit the same sort of response bias as the motivation questions. Citizen interests attribute greater importance to all but one of the factors listed in table 5.4. To correct this possible source of bias, I transformed the economic group, professional group and business responses as previously, this

---

here is theoretically justified because it reflects the ratio of citizen to economic interest mean responses. Other theoretically motivated transformations such as transforming the economic interest data by dividing each response by the respondent's individual mean response produce comparable results.

TABLE 5.4
Importance for Using Direct Legislation, Raw and Transformed Values, $\delta = 1.333244$

	Untransformed		Transformed			
Reason	Economic Professional Business	Citizen Occupational	Econ Prof Bus	Cit Occ	t	Pr > |t|
Familiar with direct legislation	3.93	4.60	5.24	4.60	1.48	.1437
	N = 55	N = 25				
Probability of qualifying initiative	2.92	3.96	3.89	3.96	−.15	.8846
	N = 50	N = 24				
Probability of passing initiative	2.92	3.96	3.89	3.96	−.15	.8840
	N = 50	N = 24				
Difficulty of using legislative process	2.78	3.88	3.71	3.88	−.38	.7018
	N = 50	N = 24				
Experience with direct legislation	3.66	4.27	4.88	4.27	1.48	.1436
	N = 56	N = 26				
Availability of consultants	2.98	3.31	3.97	3.31	1.60	.1131
	N = 53	N = 26				
Support from members	4.20	3.92	5.60	3.92	5.24	.0000
	N = 55	N = 26				
Availability of resources	3.88	4.12	5.18	4.12	3.17	.0022
	N = 52	N = 26				
Availability of volunteers	3.50	3.92	4.67	3.92	2.00	.0490
	N = 52	N = 26				

Source: Survey of interest groups (App. B).

time by a factor of 1.333244 (the ratio of citizen to economic interest mean responses over the nine items). The *t*-statistics show that economic interests attribute more importance to member support, availability of resources, and availability of volunteers. Citizen interests attribute greater importance to the probability of qualifying and passing the measure and to the difficulty of using the legislative process, although the latter differences are not statistically significant. These response patterns are consistent with the hypothesized differences in group motivations: Citizen interests are hypothesized to place more emphasis on passing new laws by initiative; therefore their success in being able to pass their measures ought to play a much greater role in their decision to use direct legislation. Economic interests are hypothesized to place less emphasis on passing new initiatives and thus place greater weight on other considerations.

I also asked nonusers why they had chosen not to pursue direct legislation. Although the subsets of economic and citizen interest nonusers are too small to allow comparisons between these group types (*n* = 49 and 15, respectively), some analysis of their aggregate responses is instructive.

IMPORTANCE FOR NOT USING DIRECT LEGISLATION

A. Never considered using direct legislation
B. Lack of familiarity with the direct legislation process
C. Low probability of qualifying an initiative or referendum
D. High cost of qualifying an initiative or referendum
E. Low probability of passing an initiative or referendum
F. High cost of a direct legislation campaign
G. Wouldn't generate enough publicity
H. Wouldn't influence the legislature's behavior
 I. Easier to influence the legislative process (i.e., state legislature)
 J. Resistance from members
K. Lack of volunteers
 L. Stringent reporting requirements
M. Other

The most frequent motivation for not using direct legislation is that influencing the state legislative process is easier (item I, mean = 3.72). Nonusers also point to the high cost of a direct legislation campaign (item F, mean = 3.25) and the high cost of qualification (item D, mean = 3.05). Many also report never considering using direct legislation (item A, mean = 3.02).

In sum, the survey data show that economic and citizen interests pursue forms of influence that reflect their relative abilities to amass monetary and personnel resources. Because they can mobilize the personnel resources required to generate an electoral majority, citizen groups seek to influence policy directly by passing new laws by initiative. Depending on how one interprets across-group differences in response patterns, the difference between economic and citizen interests in attributing importance to achieving direct modifying influence is or is not statistically significant. In addition, economic interests seek to influence policy indirectly by pressuring the legislature. Together, the patterns in these survey responses provide preliminary evidence for rejecting the null hypothesis that economic and citizen interest groups use direct legislation to achieve similar forms of influence. Indeed, their motivations reflect groups' resource advantages.

Direct Legislation Activities

The theory also posits that groups with different comparative advantages at mobilizing resources will engage in different political activities. Specifically, because of their comparative advantages, I hypothesize that citizen interests will employ strategies that require personnel resources and that economic interests will adopt strategies that require monetary resources.

In the surveys, I asked respondents to indicate the number of times over the last five years that their organization engaged in each of the direct legislation activities listed below.[12] Groups were offered the response categories 0 (Never), 1, 2–3, 4–10, and 11+.

  A. Organized your members to circulate petitions for the purpose of qualifying an initiative
  B. Made a nonfinancial contribution, such as donating staff time or resources, to an initiative or referendum campaign
  C. Made a financial contribution to an initiative or referendum campaign
  D. Lobbied the state legislature to place a referendum on the ballot
  E. Publicly endorsed or opposed an initiative or referendum
  F. Sponsored fundraising activities to support an initiative or referendum campaign
  G. Joined a ballot measure committee that was formed to support or oppose an initiative or referendum
  H. Drafted initiative legislation to be placed on a statewide ballot
  I. Other activities involving statewide initiatives or referendums

Some of these activities, such as circulating petitions (activity A) and making nonfinancial contributions (B), require personnel resources. Others, such as making financial contributions (C), require financial resources. Still others, such as lobbying the state legislature (D), publicly endorsing an initiative or referendum (E), fundraising (F), joining a campaign committee (G), and drafting initiative legislation (H), require either personnel or financial resources. Therefore, I expect citizen interests to report more often circulating petitions and making nonfinancial contributions (activities A and B) and for economic interests to report making financial contributions (activity C).

Table 5.5 reports the usage of direct legislation activities by economic interests and by citizen interests. The second and third columns show the mean number of each activity reported by groups in each category.[13] For economic interests, the most important activities are endorsing measures and joining committees. These activities require the lowest commitments of either personnel or monetary resources. Economic interests also report making financial and nonfinancial contributions as important activities. Citizen interests exhibit very different patterns of direct legislation activities. Citizen interests also report endorsing measures as their most frequent activity. Their next most frequent activity, however, is making nonfinancial contributions, followed by joining committees. These patterns reflect citizen interests' advantages at mo-

---

[12] To facilitate discussion of these responses, I omit several items in this battery and reorder others.

[13] To compute these means, I scored responses in the category "2–3" as a 2, in the category "4–10" as a 4, and in the category "11+" as an 11. This method undercounts actual usage; however, such undercounting should be the same for citizen and economic interests.

TABLE 5.5

Usage of Direct Legislation Activities by Group Type, Raw and Transformed Values, δ = 1.970213

Activity	Untransformed		Transformed			
	Econ Prof Bus	Cit Occ	Econ Prof Bus	Cit Occ	t	Pr > |t|
Circulated petitions	.42	1.80	.82	1.80	−2.17	.0314
	N = 110	N = 46				
Nonfinancial contributions	1.16	2.48	2.29	2.48	−.29	.7717
	N = 110	N = 46				
Financial contributions	1.13	1.85	2.22	1.85	.64	.5219
	N = 109	N = 46				
Lobbied	.57	1.00	1.13	1.00	.32	.7458
	N = 110	N = 42				
Endorsed	1.96	3.54	3.87	3.54	.38	.7043
	N = 110	N = 46				
Held fundraisers	.44	.75	.86	.75	.33	.7419
	N = 108	N = 44				
Joined committee	1.23	2.20	2.42	2.20	.43	.6662
	N = 109	N = 45				
Drafted measures	.19	.49	.38	.49	−.52	.6056
	N = 110	N = 45				

Source: Survey of interest groups (App. B).

bilizing personnel resources. Citizen interests report circulating petitions quite frequently as well.[14]

The transformed responses in the last four columns of table 5.5 illustrate some important differences between economic and citizen interests. Citizen interests report circulating petitions significantly more often than economic interests. This difference is significant at the .05 level. Citizen interests also report making nonfinancial contributions and drafting legislation more often than economic interests, as predicted, although these differences are not statistically significant. Economic interests report making financial contributions more often than citizen interests, although this difference is also not statistically significant.

Finally, both economic and citizen interests report engaging in the activities that require either monetary or personnel resources, as predicted. The differ-

[14] Contrary to expectations, citizen groups also report making financial contributions quite frequently. This may in part reflect my sampling procedures in which groups are sampled from the population of groups that made financial contributions to direct legislation campaigns.

ences between economic and citizen interests in lobbying the state legislature, endorsing initiatives or referendums, organizing fundraising activities, and joining committees are statistically indistinguishable.

Non-Direct Legislation Activities

I asked groups about their activities in other political arenas as well. Although my theory of interest group choice does not directly address patterns in these other political activities, I can apply the logic of the theory to say something about the non-direct legislation activities economic and citizen groups undertake. In particular, I expect economic interests to undertake political activities (in both direct legislation and other policy arenas) that require monetary resources and citizen interests to undertake direct legislation and non-direct legislation political activities that require personnel resources. Respondents were asked to indicate which of the following nondirect legislation activities they engage in.

- **A.** Contribute to campaigns for candidates to a state legislature
- **B.** Contribute to campaigns for candidates to other state offices
- **C.** Contribute to campaigns for candidates to the U.S. Congress
- **D.** Coordinate letter writing, E-mail, or telephone campaigns to inform state legislators of member policy positions
- **E.** Testify before a government commission, hearing, or other legislative session
- **F.** Employ a lobbyist to represent your organization's interests in the state legislature
- **G.** Employ a lobbyist to represent your organization's interests in the U.S. Congress
- **H.** Work with state government agencies in policy formation and implementation
- **I.** Work with federal government agencies in policy formation and implementation
- **J.** Pursue issues through litigation in the courts
- **K.** Organize protests
- **L.** Seek to influence public opinion through the use of the mass media
- **M.** Other

Table 5.6 reports the percent of groups that reported engaging in each of the twelve non-direct legislation activities. The second column reports these percentages for economic interests, and the third column reports the percentages for citizen interests. Because there is no evidence of response bias on these questions, with economic interests reporting some activities as more important

TABLE 5.6
Usage of Non-Direct Legislation Activities by Group Type, Raw Values

Activity	Economic Professional Business	Citizen Occupational	t	Pr > |t|
Contributed to state legislative candidates	.65 N = 60	.55 N = 31	.94	.3506
Contributed to other state candidates	.55 N = 60	.45 N = 31	.88	.3790
Contributed to congressional candidates	.40 N = 60	.32 N = 31	.72	.4749
Coordinated letter writing	.78 N = 59	.97 N = 31	−2.39	.0191
Testified before government agencies	.49 N = 59	.55 N = 31	−.51	.6129
Represented by lobbyist at state level	.78 N = 59	.87 N = 31	−1.05	.2983
Represented by lobbyist at federal level	.37 N = 59	.26 N = 31	1.09	.2773
Worked with state agencies	.88 N = 59	.81 N = 31	.95	.3423
Worked with federal agencies	.56 N = 59	.48 N = 31	.68	.5009
Pursued litigation	.39 N = 59	.68 N = 31	−2.67	.0091
Organized protests	.07 N = 59	.35 N = 31	−3.69	.0004
Used mass media to influence public opinion	.54 N = 59	.77 N = 31	−2.19	.0313

Source: Survey of interest groups (App. B).

and citizen interests reporting other activities as more important, I report the *t*-statistic from the difference in means test (for intergroup comparisons) on the raw responses only.

Economic interests most often report working with state agencies and employing a lobbyist to represent their interests in the state legislature.[15] They also coordinate letter-writing campaigns, contribute to state legislative candidates, hire a lobbyist to represent their interests in the U.S. Congress, work with federal agencies, and contribute to candidates for other state offices.

---

[15] The emphasis on state government may be in part an artifact of the sampling procedure, which draws nonusers from the population of contributors to candidates for statewide political office.

TABLE 5.7

Usage of Non-Direct Legislation Activities, Users and Nonusers, Raw Values

Activity	Nonusers	Users	t	$Pr > \lvert t \rvert$
Contributed to state legislative	.58	.62	−.39	.6960
candidates	N = 60	N = 91		
Contributed to other state candidates	.53	.52	.20	.8406
	N = 60	N = 91		
Contributed to congressional	.40	.37	.32	.7464
candidates	N = 60	N = 91		
Coordinated letter writing	.78	.84	−.95	.3432
	N = 60	N = 90		
Testified before government agencies	.28	.51	−2.82	.0054
	N = 60	N = 90		
Represented by lobbyist at state level	.78	.86	−1.14	.2553
	N = 60	N = 90		
Represented by lobbyist at federal	.42	.53	−1.40	.1635
level	N = 60	N = 90		
Pursued litigation	.35	.49	−1.69	.0938
	N = 60	N = 90		
Organized protests	.13	.17	−.55	.5818
	N = 60	N = 90		
Used mass media to influence public	.40	.62	−2.72	.0073
opinion	N = 60	N = 90		

Source: Survey of interest groups (App. B).

Citizen interests report very different patterns of activities. Citizen interests most often report coordinating letter-writing campaigns, hiring a lobbyist to represent them in the state legislature, working with state agencies, using the mass media to influence public opinion, and pursing issues through litigation. Comparing across groups, citizen interests more often report coordinating letter-writing campaigns, using the courts and the mass media, and organizing protests than do economic interests. All of these activities require personnel resources, and all of these differences are significant at the .05 level. Citizen interests pursue money-intensive strategies such as contributing to candidates at all levels of government and hiring a lobbyist less often than do economic interests, but these differences are not statistically significant.

Table 5.7 reports differences in non-direct legislation activities by direct legislation users and nonusers. Users more often testify before (federal) government agencies, pursue litigation, and use the mass media to influence public opinion. Nonusers more often contribute to other state candidates and to members of Congress, but not significantly more. Interestingly, these responses suggest that direct legislation users—both citizen interests and economic interests—more actively employ many forms of participatory political activities, that is, activities that require more group engagement than simply contributing to candidates for office.

To summarize, the survey evidence reveals important differences in the activities that economic and citizen groups undertake. Economic interests are more likely to engage in activities that require monetary resources, whereas citizen interests are more likely to engage in activities that require personnel resources.

What Do Groups Actually Do?

Analysis of the campaign contributions data provides further evidence that citizen and economic interest groups have different motivations and pursue different strategies. The theory predicts differences in behavior both within citizen groups and economic groups and between group types. Specifically, I hypothesize that when they can mobilize sufficient monetary resources, citizen groups will use direct legislation to achieve direct modifying influence more often than direct preserving influence. I also hypothesize that citizen groups will pursue direct modifying influence more often than do economic groups. I therefore expect to observe citizen groups contributing in favor of proposed changes to the status quo (initiatives and submitted referendums) and against attempts to preserve the status quo (popular referendums). Economic groups, by contrast, can rarely mobilize sufficient electoral support to achieve direct modifying influence, even if they have substantial monetary resources. Instead, I hypothesize that they will pursue direct preserving influence. I therefore expect to observe economic groups contributing in opposition to initiatives and submitted referendums and in support of popular referendums.

Table 5.8 reports the total contributions from economic interests and from citizen interests to all statewide ballot measures in my sample in the eight states from 1988 to 1992 (1988 and 1990 for California). The data also include information on contributions by autonomous individuals. Although individual contributors may be motivated as either autonomous individuals or as quasi-economic actors making contributions on behalf of their economic/professional/business interests, there is no way to know their motivations from the information provided in the campaign disclosure reports. I therefore include these contributions in the citizen interest category; to the extent that some of these individuals are in fact acting as economic agents, differences between the two categories will be attenuated, and my estimates will be biased against my hypotheses.[16] The lower section of table 5.8 separately reports the

---

[16] Similar patterns emerge when I exclude the contributions from autonomous individuals. Because a rather large share of all contributions come from individuals, however, I prefer to include them in the citizen interest category rather than throw away the information contained in their patterns of contributions.

TABLE 5.8
Contributions to Support and Oppose Ballot Measures

Group Type	Total	% of Total	% For	% Against
Economic	$154,265,959	68	32	68
Professional				
Business				
Citizen	55,845,207	25	74	26
Occupational				
Individual				
Business	141,750,322	62	31	69
Economic	11,936,903	5	48	52
Professional	578,734	0	46	54
Occupational	17,251,229	8	59	41
Citizen	16,751,983	7	84	16
Individual	21,841,995	10	79	21
Candidate	13,304,249	6	49	51
Indistinguishable	3,915,873	2	36	64
Total	$227,331,288	100	44	56

Sources: California: California Fair Political Practices Commission (1988a, 1988b, 1990a, 1990b); Idaho: Idaho Secretary of State (1988, 1992); Maine: State of Maine, Committee on Governmental Ethics and Election Practices (1989, 1990, 1991); Michigan: Michigan Secretary of State (1988, 1992); Missouri: Missouri Secretary of State (1988, 1990, 1991, 1992); Nebraska: Nebraska Accountability and Disclosure Commission (1988, 1990, 1992); Oregon: Oregon Secretary of State, Elections Division (1988, 1990, 1992); Washington: Washington Secretary of State (1989, 1990, 1991, 1992).

contributions from each of the contributor types plus candidates. The table also breaks down the contributions from each group type into the percentage of those contributions made in support of and in opposition to ballot measures.

The second and third columns of table 5.8 report the total contributions by each contributor type and the percentage of all contributions by each contributor type, respectively. Economic groups, professional groups, and businesses accounted for over two-thirds (68 percent) of all contributions, whereas citizen groups, occupational groups, and individuals accounted for 25 percent. The lower section of the table shows that the bulk of all contributions come directly from businesses, which accounted for over 62 percent of the $227 million in total contributions. Individuals and candidates accounted for another 16 percent.[17] Of the $46.5 million in contributions coming from organized interest groups, the greatest share was from occupational groups, who accounted for

[17] Approximately 2 percent were uncodable from the campaign finance reports. I refer to these as "Indistinguishable" in tables 5.8 and 5.9.

8 percent of the total. Citizen groups accounted for 7 percent of the total, economic groups accounted for 5 percent, and professional groups accounted for less than 1 percent. The fourth and fifth columns break down the contributions by each contributor type into contributions in support of ballot measures and contributions in opposition to ballot measures.[18]

Columns 4 and 5 show that economic interests dedicate a substantially greater proportion of their contributions to campaigns to defeat changes to the status quo. Sixty-eight percent of the contributions from economic interests go to opposition campaigns, whereas only 26 percent of contributions from citizen interests go to opposition campaigns. By contrast, citizen interests contribute a far greater share of their contributions—nearly three-quarters—to support initiatives and submitted referendums. The lower portion of table 5.8 breaks down these percentages by individual contributor types. Here, we see that all types of economic interests—businesses, professional groups, and economic groups—contribute more to opposition campaigns than to supporting campaigns. All types of citizen interests—citizen groups, occupational groups, and individuals—contribute more to supporting campaigns. Together, these patterns show that citizen interests direct a far greater proportion of their contributions toward achieving modifying influence, as hypothesized, whereas economic interests spend a greater proportion on achieving preserving influence. I take this as compelling evidence that economic and citizen interests pursue different forms of influence when they use direct legislation.

I further hypothesize that economic and citizen interests will pursue different contribution strategies on initiatives and submitted referendums.[19] Economic interests may have better access to the legislature because of their monetary resources but less appeal to the mass electorate. I therefore expect them to support referendums that are produced by their allies in the legislature and to oppose initiatives that circumvent the legislative process. Citizen interests have less access to the legislature but greater electoral support. I therefore expect them to support initiatives as an alternative to legislative politics and to oppose referendums placed on the ballot by the legislature.

Table 5.9 reports the contributions to support and oppose initiatives and referendums by contributor type. Columns 2 to 4 report contributions made to initiative campaigns. Columns 5 to 7 report contributions made to referendum campaigns.

As hypothesized, economic interest groups, professional groups and businesses direct a greater share of their contributions to opposing (74 percent)

[18] Note that this includes contributions for and against both initiatives and referendums. Because all of the referendums in the sample are submitted referendums, contributions in favor of those measures, like contributions in favor of initiatives, represent support for a change in the status quo. In other words, all supporting contributions in this table are contributions to support change, whereas all opposing contributions are contributions to oppose change.

[19] All of the referendums in the sample are submitted referendums that were automatically placed on the ballot by the legislature.

TABLE 5.9

Contributions to Support and Oppose Initiatives and Referendums

	To Initiatives			To Referendums		
Group Type	Total	Support (%)	Oppose (%)	Total	Support (%)	Oppose (%)
Economic Professional Business	$141,067,159	26	74	$13,198,800	98	2
Citizen Occupational Individual	51,115,046	72	28	4,730,161	92	8
Business	130,543,029	25	75	11,207,293	98	2
Economic	9,975,246	38	62	1,961,657	98	2
Professional	548,884	43	57	29,850	100	0
Occupational	15,947,109	55	45	1,304,120	98	2
Citizen	14,128,550	81	19	2,623,433	99	1
Individual	21,039,387	80	20	802,608	57	43
Candidate	12,497,182	45	55	807,067	99	1
Indistinguishable	3,682,606	33	67	233,267	98	2
Total	$208,361,993	39	61	$18,969,295	97	3

Sources: See table 5.8.

rather than to supporting (26 percent) initiatives and a greater share of their contributions to supporting (98 percent) rather than opposing (2 percent) referendums. Citizen groups, occupational groups, and individuals direct a greater share to supporting (72 percent) rather than opposing (28 percent) initiatives. Although they also report spending more to support rather than oppose referendums, their share of supporting contributions to referendums (92 percent) is quite a bit lower than the share by economic interests (98 percent). These differences aside, however, and independent of my hypotheses, it is interesting to note that, although economic interests devote a much lower *share* of their initiative contributions to supporting initiative measures than do citizen interests, the *absolute amount* of the contributions made to support initiative measures by economic interests ($36,888,333) is nearly identical to the amount of the contributions made to support initiative measures by citizen interests ($37,053,207). In other words, the two types of groups provide equal support for initiative measures.

In the detailed breakdown in the lower section of table 5.9, we see that the greater the contributor's posited advantage at mobilizing personnel resources (which increases as we move down the lower section of the table), the higher the percentage of contributions to support initiatives and the lower the percentage of contributions to oppose initiatives. Businesses contribute only 25 percent of their initiative contributions to supporting initiative measures. Economic groups contribute 38 percent to support initiatives, professional groups 43 percent, occupational groups 55 percent, citizen groups 81 percent, and individuals 80 percent.[20] Candidates, for which the theory produces no specific predictions, split their contributions between support and opposition, with slightly more going toward opposition.

By contrast, all contributor types except autonomous individuals contribute a much larger share of the contributions they make to referendum campaigns to supporting the measures. Two aspects of these referendum contributions figures warrant further mention. First, all contributor types direct a much lower share of their contributions to referendums than they do to initiatives. The highest share of referendum contributions comes from economic groups and citizen groups, both of which contribute 16 percent of their total contributions to referendum campaigns. Although we expect economic groups to support submitted referendums, the high level of financial contributions to referendum campaigns made by citizen groups, especially relative to other groups, is contrary to my expectations. Second, there is very little opposition to the referendums in this data set, accounting for only 3 percent of the contributions to all referendum campaigns and only .03 percent of all contributions to all direct legislation campaigns in the eight states during the six-year period. This absence of opposition spending suggests that compromises are struck in the legislative phase of the referendum process that mitigate opposition at the ballot box.

To summarize, preliminary analysis of the campaign contributions data suggests that economic interests and citizen interests pursue different forms of influence when they make financial contributions to direct legislation campaigns. Citizen groups, occupational groups, and individuals spend a large share of their financial contributions to promote initiatives. They also spend a greater share on opposing referendums. Economic groups, professional groups, and businesses spend a large share of their financial contributions to oppose initiatives and to support referendums. These patterns are broadly consistent with the hypotheses that citizen groups pursue modifying influence more often than preserving influence and that they pursue modifying influence more often than do economic groups. Economic groups pursue preserving influence more often than modifying influence and pursue preserving influence more often than do citizen groups.

The second set of analyses in this section considers the subject areas of the measures to which economic groups and citizen groups contribute. Table 5.10

---

[20] There is a small reversal in this pattern as we move from citizen groups to individuals, suggesting that some organizational representatives are, as suspected, included in the "Individuals" category. This deviation from the expected pattern is very small, however.

TABLE 5.10
Contributions from Contributor Types by Subject Areas

Subject Area	Contributions from Economic, Professional, Business			Contributions from Citizen, Occupational, Individual		
	Total (%)	Support (%)	Oppose (%)	Total (%)	Support (%)	Oppose (%)
Revenue & Tax	26	19	30	13	7	32
Environment	21	14	24	22	28	5
Health & Welfare	18	8	23	15	12	23
Business & Labor Regulations	13	15	12	2	2	4
Transportation	10	20	5	4	5	1
Government & Political Process	5	11	2	20	21	18
Civil Rights/Civil Liberties	3	0	4	1	0	2
Education	2	6	0	15	20	3
Corrections	2	6	0	3	4	2
Gambling/Morality	1	1	1	3	1	9
Total[a]	101	100	101	99	100	99

Sources: See table 5.8.

[a] Does not sum to 100% because of rounding.

categorizes each of the 161 ballot measures by its primary subject area and then reports the distribution of economic group, professional group, and business contributions and of citizen group, occupational group, and individual contributions across those subject areas.[21] Although the theory does not directly produce hypotheses about the subject areas that different groups will pursue, patterns of contributions by group types will provide further insight into the ways contributors use the direct legislation process.

Table 5.10 shows that economic interests and citizen interests concentrate their resources on different issue areas. The second column shows that economic interests contribute the greatest share of their total contributions, 26 percent, to revenue and taxation measures. Economic interests also direct a large share of their total contributions to measures dealing with the environ-

---

[21] I exclude the five 1988 California insurance initiatives (Propositions 100, 101, 103, 104, and 106) from this and subsequent analyses because some of the ballot measure committees were formed to support and/or oppose multiple measures (e.g., "Californians against Unfair Increases No on Prop 100 and 103"), whereas others transferred substantial sums between committees ("Citizens for No Fault Sponsored by CA Insurers," supporters of Proposition 104, transferred nearly $2.8 million to "Committee for Fair Lawyers Fees Sponsored by Insurance Industries," supporters of Proposition 106), making it impossible to isolate which contributions were directed toward which campaigns. These measures together also accounted for over $100 million in total spending, so that their inclusion would potentially swamp many other important patterns (California Fair Political Practices Commission 1988b).

TABLE 5.11

Contributions to Subject Areas by Contributor Type

Contributions To	Economic Professional Business (%)	Citizen Occupational Individual (%)	Other (%)	Total
Government & Political Process	24	37	39	$30,971,858
Revenue & Tax	83	15	1	49,001,768
Business & Labor Regulations	94	6	0	21,509,727
Health & Welfare	75	23	2	36,689,953
Environment	69	27	3	46,185,660
Civil Rights/Civil Liberties	88	11	1	4,508,092
Education	25	69	6	12,420,325
Transportation	85	12	3	17,554,173
Corrections	54	34	13	5,579,121
Gambling/Morality	38	61	1	2,910,611

Sources: See table 5.8.

ment, health and welfare, and business and labor regulation. They concentrate their supporting contributions on revenue and taxation and transportation measures (column 3) and their opposition contributions on revenue and tax, environmental, and health and welfare measures (column 4). Citizen interests contribute to different sorts of measures. The fifth column of table 5.10 shows that citizen interests dedicate the highest percentage (22 percent) of their total contributions to environmental measures, 20 percent to government and political process measures, 15 percent each to health and welfare and education measures, and 13 percent to revenue and taxation measures. Citizen interests spend the greatest share of their supporting contributions on environmental, government and political process, and education measures and the greatest share of their opposition contributions on revenue and taxation, health and welfare, and government and political process measures.

Table 5.11 presents the contribution data by subject area in a slightly different format. The three middle columns of table 5.11 report the percentage of all contributions to measures in each subject area by economic groups, professional groups, and businesses; citizen groups, occupational groups, and individuals; and other contributors. The last column of table 5.11 reports the total contributions to measures in each subject area. Thus, the first row shows that economic interests accounted for 24 percent of the $30,971,858 in contributions to government and political process measures, citizen interests accounted for 37 percent; and other contributors (primarily candidates) accounted for 39 percent.

Economic interests accounted for the largest share of contributions to revenue and taxation measures (83 percent); business and labor regulation measures (94 percent); health and welfare measures (75 percent); environmental measures (69 percent); civil rights/civil liberties measures (88 percent); transportation measures (85 percent); and corrections measures (54 percent). Citizen interests accounted for the largest share of contributions to education (69 percent) and gambling/public morality (61 percent) measures. Other contributors, especially candidates, accounted for the largest share of contributions to government and political process measures (39 percent).

Summary and Conclusions

Analysis of survey and campaign finance data shows that economic interests and citizen interests are motivated by different objectives and pursue different political activities to meet those objectives. As predicted by the theory, economic interests use direct legislation less often to pass laws by initiative and more often to preserve the status quo or to pressure the legislature. To do so, they undertake activities that require monetary resources. Citizen interests, by contrast, use direct legislation more often to pass laws by initiative. They undertake activities that require personnel resources.

These results have important implications for the policy consequences of interest group involvement in the direct legislation process. To the extent that economic groups and citizen groups undertake different activities and pursue different forms of influence, we expect their behavior to be reflected in policy. The next two chapters explore these effects. In chapter 6, I consider the consequences of interest group choice on the policies that result directly from the direct legislation process. In chapter 7, I consider the consequences of interest group choice on the overall mix of policies in direct legislation and non-direct legislation states.

6

Direct Policy Consequences

IN THE PRECEDING five chapters, I developed and tested my theory of interest group choice. I found that economic interest groups, professional groups, and businesses employ strategies that are more cash-intensive and less personnel-intensive. These economic interests place greater emphasis on pressuring the legislature and blocking legislation and less emphasis on passing new initiatives. Citizen interest groups, occupational groups, and autonomous individuals, by contrast, employ strategies that are more labor-intensive and less cash-intensive. They pursue direct modifying influence and place greater emphasis on passing new initiatives.

Although these behavioral differences provide new insight into how and why economic and citizen interests use the direct legislation process, such behaviors have important policy consequences only insofar as they translate into systematic differences in outcomes. In this regard, several important empirical questions remain unanswered. Do the laws that actually pass as initiatives and referendums reflect the interests of citizen groups? Do the laws that fail reflect the interests of economic groups? Do the laws passed by legislatures in initiative states reflect the pressure of citizen and economic interests? In short, do the policy outcomes resulting from both the direct legislation process and the state legislative process reflect the activities and objectives of the groups that use direct legislation?

In the next two chapters, I assess these direct and indirect policy consequences. In the remainder of this chapter, I consider the direct policy consequences of interest group choice on the laws that result from the direct legislation process. In chapter 7, I consider the indirect policy consequences.

Direct Policy Consequences

My analysis of direct consequences involves testing the extent to which policy outcomes resulting from the direct legislation process reflect the motivations and activities of groups that use initiatives and referendums. At first blush, this task appears relatively straightforward: Simply consider the set of initiatives and referendums that passed and ask whether they reflect citizen group interests, then consider the set of initiatives and referendums that failed and ask whether they reflect economic group interests. Several factors complicate this analysis, however. These factors relate to how we determine whose interests are reflected in a given ballot measure. Initiatives and referendums, like regular legislative bills, tend to be technical, far-reaching, and complex. The average length of the California statewide initiatives included in my study of contributions to direct legislation campaigns was 4,511 words, with four (Proposition 70 of 1988 and Propositions 128, 130, and 131 of 1990) containing over 10,000 words each (California Commission on Campaign Financing 1992, p. 86). These complex measures are likely to have wide-reaching consequences, affecting diverse interests in many different ways. Thus, a given measure may benefit multiple interests including both citizen groups and economic groups, or it may advantage some economic groups at the expense of others, or it may advantage some citizen groups at the expense of others. In other words, categorizing each measure as either pro-economic or pro-citizen is overly simplistic. Rather, a continuum from predominantly pro-economic to predominantly pro-citizen more accurately reflects the range of interests served by initiatives and referendums. This point is substantiated by the fact that, of the 161 initiatives and referendums included in my study of campaign contributions, only 5 received all of their support from economic interests, and only 4 received all of their support from citizen interests.[1] In other words, nearly all of the measures in this sample received some contributions from economic groups, professional groups, or businesses, and some contributions from citizen groups, occupational groups, or individuals. This pattern of financial support and opposition from diverse interests is reflected in figures 6.1 and 6.2, respectively.

In figure 6.1, measures that received all of their supporting contributions from citizen interests are plotted at point (0,1) on the vertical axis. Measures that received all of their supporting contributions from economic interests are plotted at (1,0) on the horizontal axis. Measures that received all of their contributions from either citizen or economic interests fall along the diagonal connecting these two extreme cases, and measures that received support from other contributors fall below the diagonal. Figure 6.2 reports sources of opposition spending in a similar fashion.

These figures clearly show that, although some measures are clustered near the two endpoints, many initiatives and referendums in the sample received funding from multiple sources. Admittedly, some of this apparent multiplicity of funding may be due to misclassification of the contributors. Most importantly, many of the contributions from citizen interests to measures predominantly supported by economic interests were from autonomous individuals. These individuals may be motivated by either economic or citizen interests

---

[1] Only four measures received all of their opposition from economic interests, and four received all of their opposition from citizen interests.

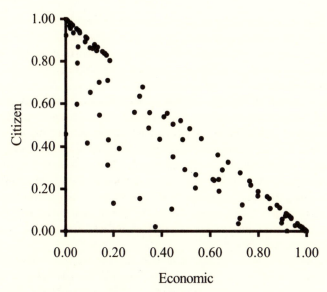

Fig. 6.1. Percent of Support from Economic and Citizen Interests

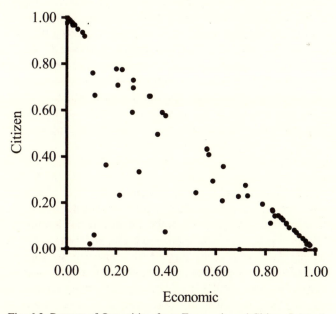

Fig. 6.2. Percent of Opposition from Economic and Citizen Interests

and therefore may be misclassified as pursuing citizen interests when their motivations were in fact economic.[2] Even with some misclassification, it is nevertheless clear that measures should not be categorized simply as economic-supported or citizen-supported, but rather by the relative support from these various interests.

Furthermore, not only length and complexity make it difficult to anticipate whose interests a ballot measure will ultimately serve. Because initiatives and referendums deal with difficult issues of social, economic, and political regulation, and because public policies are adopted and implemented in an environment of great uncertainty, it is often extremely difficult to anticipate the ultimate consequences of even the most concise and apparently straightforward ballot measures. Hence, a measure that appears to be pro-economic before passage may in fact appear quite different after implementation. Similarly, groups may differ (at any time in the policy process) over whose interests a given ballot measure serves.

In sum, because of the intricacy of most initiatives and referendums and the diverse interests they reflect, it is neither practical nor advisable to categorize measures as pro-economic or pro-citizen. Rather, I employ two different approaches to assessing whose interests a given ballot measure reflects. My first and primary approach is to analyze sources of financial support to the campaigns for and against each ballot measure in my study. Sources of financial support and opposition reflect how groups perceived the ballot measures and whose interests they believed would be served before the election. By analyzing sources of support and opposition, I am able to capture the many different interests reflected in each measure. The disadvantage to this approach is that citizen interests are less likely than economic interests to rely on monetary resources, and therefore patterns of financial contributions may overstate support from economic interests and understate support from citizen interests.

My second approach to assessing whose interests are reflected in a given ballot measure is to categorize measures by subject area. As shown in table 5.10, economic interests tend to pursue policies in the areas of transportation, revenue and taxation, business and labor regulation, and the environment. Citizen interests tend to pursue policies in the areas of the environment, government and political processes, education, and health and welfare. Because subject area is correlated with group support for a measure, we can interpret a measure's subject area as an indicator of the interests it reflects. In other words, we can infer that measures in the areas of transportation, revenue and taxation, and business and labor regulation are more likely to reflect economic interests,

[2] As discussed in chapter 5, individuals may contribute either as autonomous individuals or as economic agents. To the extent that they contribute to direct legislation campaigns to promote their business interests, as opposed to their citizen interests, the distinctions between contributor types becomes less stark.

and measures in the areas of government and political processes, education, and health and welfare are more likely to reflect citizen interests.[3] Clearly, this subject-area approach to assessing whose interests are reflected in a given ballot measure is rather imprecise; it ignores both the multiplicity of interests reflected in a given ballot measure and the fact that pursuit of policies in a given subject area is not exclusive to a particular type of group. Inferring interests from a measure's subject area does have the advantage of being based on criteria other than the sources of financial contributions to direct legislation campaigns and therefore may avoid some of the problems introduced by the reliance of citizen interests on nonfinancial sources of support or opposition.

By analyzing the sources of support and opposition and the subject areas of each initiative and referendum, I am able to assess the relative impact of economic and citizen group involvement on direct legislation outcomes. The analysis proceeds in four stages. Together, these four sets of analyses allow me to test the extent that support or opposition from citizen and economic interests translates into policy.

First, I ask, What is the effect of financial support from economic interests and citizen interests on a given measure's success? In the theoretical discussion in chapters 1 through 4, I argued that, because of their membership base and the dynamics of direct legislation campaigns, citizen groups typically only need to mobilize existing support for their measure. Mobilizing support is relatively inexpensive and allows citizen groups to pursue direct modifying influence at low cost. Economic groups, by contrast, typically need to persuade large numbers of voters and therefore can achieve direct modifying influence only at high cost. Together, these premises about groups' comparative advantages imply that a dollar spent by citizen groups translates more readily into policy success than a dollar spent by economic groups. To test this hypothesis, I compare the effects of spending by economic interests and by citizen interests on a measure's success. I find evidence that, although citizen groups cannot necessarily translate financial support into direct modifying influence, economic groups have even more difficulty doing so. In fact, a dollar spent by economic groups to support initiatives and referendums translates into a lower vote margin and probability of passage, all other things being equal.

The second question is, What is the impact of financial support from economic interests and citizen interests on aggregate passage rates? I address this question in two ways. I first compare the passage rates for measures that received majority and supermajority support from economic interests with the passage rates for measures that received majority and supermajority support from citizen interests. To the extent that citizen interests are better able to

---

[3] Because both citizen and economic interests pursue environmental measures, inferences about whose interests those measures reflect are ambiguous.

achieve direct modifying influence, I expect measures that receive substantial support from them to pass at a higher rate than measures that receive most of their support from economic interests. The analysis provides suppport for these hypotheses: Measures that receive majority support from citizen interests pass at a significantly higher rate than those that receive majority support from economic interests; measures that receive supermajority support from citizen interests also pass at a higher rate, but the difference is not significant.

Next, I analyze whether successful initiatives receive a greater share of their supporting contributions from citizen interests and whether unsuccessful initiatives receive a greater share of their support from economic interests. I find evidence that successful initiatives receive a much greater share of their support from citizen interests. I find, however, that unsuccessful initiatives also receive a greater share of their support from citizen interests, contrary to expectations.

The third question is, What is the effect of financial opposition from economic and citizen interests on a given measure's success and on aggregate passage rates? Whereas the analyses above show that economic interests are less able than citizen interests to achieve direct modifying influence, an important part of my argument is that, instead, economic interests can more easily achieve direct preserving influence. Therefore, I perform parallel analyses considering the effects of financial opposition by economic and citizen interests. In each case, I find evidence that economic interests are better able to block initiatives than are citizen interests: Opposition spending by economic interests is related to a larger decrease in a measure's vote margin and probability of passage; initiatives that receive majority and supermajority opposition from economic interests pass at a lower rate than those that receive majority and supermajority opposition from citizen interests; and unsuccessful initiatives receive a greater share of their opposition from economic interests.

Finally, I ask, Do successful and unsuccessful initiatives and referendums reflect different issues? Because citizen and economic interests tend to pursue policies in different issue areas, I expect initiatives and referendums in the issue areas that citizen groups focus on to pass at a higher rate. I further expect successful initiatives and referendums to reflect the substantive concerns of citizen interest groups and unsuccessful measures to reflect the substantive concerns of economic groups. I find evidence supportive of these hypotheses: Initiatives and referendums in the areas most often pursued by citizen interests pass at the highest rates, and those in the areas most often pursued by economic interests pass at much lower rates. In addition, measures in the subject areas most often pursued by citizen interests account for the greatest share of successful initiatives and referendums, and measures in the subject areas most often pursued by economic interests account for the greatest share of unsuccessful initiatives and referendums.

Financial Support and Policy Success

I first assess the effect of financial support from different groups on a measure's success. This part of the study involves analyzing campaign contributions to the 161 ballot measures described in chapter 5. I first estimate the effect of contributions made by different types of groups on the measure's vote margin. The unit of analysis is a single measure; the dependent variable is the difference between the number of votes cast for and against the measure; and the independent variables are the dollars spent by each group type to support the measure plus several control variables.[4] For this part of the analysis, I drop the thirty-two measures for which no supporting or opposing contributions were reported. I also drop the five 1988 California insurance measures because of severe coding problems.[5] Because vote margin is a continuous variable, ranging from −6,793,924 to +4,319,213, I estimate the model using standard ordinary least squares (OLS) regression.

The second column of table 6.1 reports the bivariate relationship between contributions from economic groups, professional groups, and businesses and the measure's vote margin. The negative, strong, and significant relationship suggests that contributions from economic interests are associated with a lower vote margin, as hypothesized. In other words, the measure's success as measured by its vote margin decreases as economic interests provide greater financial support for the measure. Column three reports the relationship between contributions from citizen groups, occupational groups, and individuals and the measure's vote margin. This relationship is also negative, contrary to expectations, indicating that the measure's vote margin also decreases as citizen interests provide greater support for the measure. This effect is not statistically significant, however.

Subsequent columns of table 6.1 report the results of multivariate analyses that include contributions from both economic and citizen interests, plus additional variables that indicate whether the measure was an initiative, the level of net spending, whether the opposition waged a large campaign (over $1 million) against the measure, and a set of state dummy variables. These multivariate analyses allow me to estimate the independent effect of each variable on a measure's vote margin, controlling for the effects of the other included variables. We see that, under each specification, the effect of contributions

---

[4] I also ran the vote margin analysis using percentages rather than number of votes. This analysis produced comparable but slightly weaker results. Supplemental analyses are available upon request from the author.

[5] Several of the committees formed to support or oppose these measures directed resources to campaigns for or against more than one measure. It is therefore impossible to allocate these contributions (and their effects) accurately to a single measure. For more on this particular election, see Lupia (1994).

TABLE 6.1
Effect of Supporting Contributions on Vote Margin, Regression Estimates

Independent Variables	Estimated Effects–Regression Coefficients[a]						
Constant	.14 (.10)	.09 (.10)	.18* (.11)	.52** (.16)	.51** (.15)	.51** (.15)	.64** (.20)
Economic	−.24** (.09)		−.24** (.09)	−.22** (.09)	−.27** (.09)	−.21** (.09)	−.27** (.09)
Citizen		−.12 (.11)	−.12 (.11)	−.06 (.11)	−.05 (.11)	.00 (.11)	−.03 (.12)
Initiative				−.57** (.19)	−.51** (.19)	−.46** (.20)	−.54** (.22)
NetSpend					.05** (.03)		
BigNo						−.57** (.27)	−.70** (.27)
Idaho							−.48 (.59)
Maine							−.17 (.48)
Michigan							1.13** (.41)
Missouri							−.19 (.30)
Nebraska							−.24 (.33)
Oregon							−.04 (.27)
Washington							−.23 (.38)
N	125	125	125	125	125	125	125
Adjusted R^2	.04	.00	.05	.10	.12	.13	.15

Sources: See table 5.8.
[a] Standard errors are in parentheses.   * $p < .10$ ** $p < .05$

from economic interests is negative and significant. The effect of contributions from citizen interests is negative and insignificant when we control for contributions from economic interests, whether the measure was an initiative, and the level of net spending. The effect is positive but not significant when we account for whether there was a large campaign waged against the measure.[6] These results become slightly stronger when we also include a set of dummy variables for each state, with California as the excluded category.

These regression results provide preliminary evidence that financial support from citizen interests translates more readily into votes than financial support from economic interests. From these results alone, however, it is not clear that the effects of citizen and economic group support necessarily translate into differences in policy. It may be the case, for example, that, although support from economic groups results in a lower vote margin, the baseline vote margin for these measures is so low that they are very likely to fail anyway. Or it may be the case that the baseline vote margin on many measures is sufficiently high that even reducing the vote margin by a substantial amount does not affect ultimate passage rates.[7] Therefore, in addition to analyzing the effect of con-

[6] Because *BigNo* and *NetSpend* are created from essentially the same data, I include only one of these variables at a time in the multivariate analysis to avoid severe multicollinearity.
[7] The notion that measures supported by economic and citizen groups may have different baseline vote margins implies some degree of simultaneity between the types of contributors that

TABLE 6.2

Effect of Supporting Contributions on Probability of Passage, Logit Estimates

Independent Variables	Estimated Effects–Logit Coefficients[a]						
Constant	.03* (.02)	.03 (.02)	.04* (.02)	.12** (.04)	.12** (.04)	.12** (.04)	.14** (.05)
Economic	−.32 (.21)		−.32 (.21)	−.29 (.22)	−.42* (.24)	−.29 (.22)	−.41* (.23)
Citizen		−.14 (.21)	−.14 (.21)	−.00 (.21)	.00 (.23)	.23 (.25)	.11 (.28)
Initiative				−.13** (.04)	−.12** (.04)	−.10** (.04)	−.08* (.05)
NetSpend					.14 (.11)		
BigNo						−.21** (.07)	−.25** (.08)
Idaho							−.04 (.13)
Maine							.07 (.12)
Michigan							.24* (.13)
Missouri							−.05 (.07)
Nebraska							.04 (.08)
Oregon							−.10* (.06)
Washington							−.14* (.08)
N	125	125	125	125	125	125	125
Pseudo R^2	.02	.00	.02	.08	.09	.14	.21

Sources: See table 5.8.

[a] Asymptotic standard errors are in parentheses.   * $p < .10$ ** $p < .05$

tributions from different types of groups on a measure's vote margin, I also estimate their effect on a measure's probability of passage. The dependent variable in this next analysis is a dummy variable scored one if the measure passed and scored zero otherwise. Because passage is a binary variable (either the measured passed or it did not), I estimate the model as a logistic regression. Table 6.2 reports these logit estimates. The estimates tell us the effect of a unit increase in each independent variable on the log of the odds ratio, that is, on $\ln(P_i/1 - P_i)$, where P_i is the probability that measure i passes, controlling for the effects of the other independent variables. Although the magnitudes of the logit coefficients are difficult to interpret without further evaluation, the significance and sign of the estimates give some idea of the effect of each independent variable on the probability of passage.

The results from the logit analysis are similar to, but somewhat weaker than, the results from the regression analysis above. Table 6.2 reports that, under each specification, there is a negative relationship between contributions from

support a measure and ultimate votes. For example, if economic groups support measures that involve greater changes in policy from the status quo, then those measures will receive greater support from economic interests *and* fewer votes, independent of any campaign effects. For the purposes of this analysis, I limit my inquiry to establishing empirically whether measures supported by economic interests receive fewer votes and disregard the question of whether these differences are due to campaign effects or simply the measure's content.

economic groups, professional groups, and businesses and the probability of passage. This effect is significant when we control for whether the measure is an initiative, net spending or the presence of a large opposition campaign, and state effects. Table 6.2 shows a small negative or positive relationship between contributions from citizen groups, occupational groups, and individuals and the probability of passage, depending on the model's specification, although none of these effects is significant. As in the regression analyses, whether the measure is an initiative and whether the opposition waged a large campaign both lower the probability of passage. Again, as in the regression analyses, accounting for state-specific differences in passage rates strengthens the results. Finally, the somewhat weaker logit results (in terms of statistical significance) provide some evidence that, although spending may affect vote margin, the change in vote margin is in some cases not enough to affect whether the measure ultimately passes or fails.

In sum, the estimates in tables 6.1 and 6.2 suggest that, although contributions from citizen groups are largely unrelated to a measure's success, contributions from economic groups are clearly associated with a lower vote margin and a lower probability of success. From these econometric results alone, however, it is not possible to infer the causal direction of these relationships. It may be that the causal arrow runs from spending to success: Spending by economic interests signals to voters that the measure is contrary to their interests and leads them to vote against the measure. Alternatively, the causal arrow may run from success (or expected success) to spending: Economic interests know that their measures are unlikely to draw much public support in the absence of a costly persuasion campaign and thus must spend a great amount of resources to have any chance of success. Both of these effects are probably important, and both are consistent with the dynamics of direct legislation campaigns and the comparative advantages of citizen and economic groups described in chapters 1 through 4. In either case, these findings are consistent with the theoretical result that citizen groups pursue direct modifying influence because they can translate resources into an electoral majority, whereas economic groups may be unable to do so, even at very great cost.

Financial Support and Passage Rates

My second test of the direct policy consequences of interest group choice investigates the relationship between financial support from citizen and economic interests and aggregate passage rates. To the extent that citizen interests can more easily pursue direct modifying influence, I expect the measures that receive a large share of their support from citizen interests to pass at a higher rate than those that receive a large share of their support from economic interests. I also expect successful measures to reflect greater support from citizen interests and unsuccessful measures to reflect greater support from economic

TABLE 6.3

Passage Rates of Initiatives with Majority and Supermajority
Support from Economic Interests, Citizen Interests, and Other
Contributors

Source of Support	Passage Rate (%)		
	50% Majority	*60% Majority*	*67% Majority*
Economic	31**	31	30
Professional	$N = 29$	$N = 26$	$N = 23$
Business			
Citizen	50**	46	46
Occupational	$N = 44$	$N = 37$	$N = 35$
Individual			
Other contributors	43	40	25
	$N = 14$	$N = 5$	$N = 4$

Sources: See table 5.8.
** Two-sample test of proportions: $H_0: \pi_e - \pi_c = \text{diff} = 0$; $H_a: \text{diff} < 0$, $P < z = .05$; $H_a: \text{diff} \neq 0$, $P < z = .11$.

interests. To test these hypotheses, I again analyze the 161 measures in my sample. I first compare the passage rates of initiatives that received majority and supermajority support from different types of groups. Note that I only include initiatives in this analysis; initiatives and referendums pass at different rates, and combining them may conflate two very different processes.[8] I report these passage rates in table 6.3.[9]

The first two rows of table 6.3 show that initiatives that received majority support from economic interests passed at a substantially lower rate than measures that received majority support from citizen interests. Thirty one percent of the measures that received majority support from economic interests passed. Fifty percent of the measures that received majority support from citizen interests passed. These differences in passage rates also hold when we look at higher levels of support (60 percent and 67 percent) from each group type. For economic interests, passage rates remain virtually unchanged when we consider supermajority support. Initiatives that received 60 percent or greater support from economic interests passed at a 31 percent rate and those that received 67 percent or greater support passed at a 30 percent rate. For citizen interests, passage rates change marginally when we consider supermajority support.

[8] Because referendums often receive majority support from economic interests and referendums pass at a higher rate than initiatives, the combined set of measures reflects this asymmetry. I report comparable results to tables 6.3 and 6.4 for referendums below.
[9] Note that in this table the percentage of measures with majority support from economic interests plus citizen interests plus other contributors does not sum to eighty-seven (the total number of initiatives). This is because some measures received a plurality (but not a majority) of support from groups in several categories.

Initiatives that received either 60 percent or 67 percent (or greater) support from citizen interests passed at a 46 percent rate.[10] A difference-of-proportions test shows that the difference in passage rates between economic-and citizen-majority-supported initiatives is statistically significant, whereas the difference in passage rates between supermajority-supported initiatives is just below standard levels of significance. I take these results as evidence that, as expected, measures supported predominantly by economic interests pass at a substantially lower rate than those supported predominantly by citizen interests.

I further investigate the relationship between success and contributions from economic and citizen interests by comparing the percentage of contributions from each contributor type in support of successful and unsuccessful initiatives. Table 6.4 reports these percentages. The second column reports the percentage of contributions from each contributor type to successful initiatives, and the third column reports the percentage of contributions from each source to unsuccessful initiatives. Again, because initiatives and referendums pass at different rates, figures are for initiatives only.

The first four rows of table 6.4 show the aggregate contributions from economic interests, citizen interests, and other contributors. In the nine bottom rows, I disaggregate those figures to show the breakdown of contributions from each separate contributor type to successful and unsuccessful initiatives. We see from table 6.4 that the set of successful initiatives received a much greater share of their supporting contributions from citizen interests. The second column shows that the set of successful initiatives received 33 percent of their supporting contributions from economic interests, 54 percent from citizen interests, and 13 percent from other contributor types. The unsuccessful measures received a greater share of their contributions from economic interests, who accounted for over 40 percent of all supporting contributions to unsuccessful measures. Unsuccessful measures received 48 percent of their supporting contributions from citizen interests and 12 percent from other contributors. Note that, although both successful and unsuccessful measures received a greater share of their supporting contributions from citizen interests than from economic interests, those that passed received a larger share (54 percent) from citizen interests.[11]

The lower section of table 6.4 breaks down sources of support by each contributor type. We see that businesses accounted for the largest share of

[10] Referendums that received majority support from economic interests passed at an 83 percent rate, whereas those that received majority support from citizen interests passed at a 50 percent rate. Note, however, that only eight referendums received majority citizen support, making this result unreliable. Referendums that received supermajority (67 percent) support from economic interests passed at an 84 percent rate, whereas those that received supermajority support from citizen interests passed at a 43 percent rate.

[11] For referendums, the results run in the opposite direction. Successful referendums received 41 percent of their support from economic interests and only 12 percent from citizen interests. Unsuccessful referendums received 25 percent of their support from economic interests and 22 percent from citizen interests.

TABLE 6.4
Sources of Support to Successful and Unsuccessful
Initiatives

Source of Support	Successful Initiatives (%)	Unsuccessful Initiatives (%)
Economic Professional Business	33[a]	40
Citizen Occupational Individual	54	48
Other Contributors	13	12
Total	100	100
Economic	5	4
Professional	1	3
Business	28	33
Citizen	21	18
Occupational	6	4
Individual	27	26
Candidate	7	3
Other	5	9
Total	100	100

Sources: See table 5.8.
[a] Discrepancies between top and bottom sections due to rounding.

contributions from economic interests. Businesses accounted for 28 percent of supporting contributions to successful initiatives and 33 percent of supporting contributions to unsuccessful initiatives. Autonomous individuals accounted for the largest share of supporting contributions from citizen interests, with citizen interest groups also accounting for a rather large share (21 percent of supporting contributions to successful initiatives; 18 percent of supporting contributions to unsuccessful initiatives). These patterns, like the patterns of aggregate contributions reported in the top section of table 6.4, are consistent with the theory.

Financial Opposition, Policy Success, and Passage Rates

The next set of analyses considers the ability of economic and citizen interests to achieve direct preserving influence. A crucial part of my argument is that, although economic interests are limited in their ability to pass new laws by

TABLE 6.5

Effect of Opposing Contributions on Vote Margin and Probability
of Passage

Independent Variables	Estimated Effects[a]	
	Vote Margin–Regression Coefficients	Probability of Passage–Logit Coefficients
Constant	.06 (.31)	1.83* (1.08)
Economic	−.06** (.03)	−.11 (.10)
Citizen	−.00 (.26)	−.01 (.08)
Initiative	−.06 (.34)	−1.75 (1.14)
BigNo	−.26 (.29)	−.66 (1.29)
BigYes	−.52** (.26)	−.33 (.72)
N	65	65
Adjusted R^2	.19	.20[b]

Sources: See table 5.8.

[a] Asymptotic standard errors are in parentheses.

[b] Pseudo-R^2.

* $p < .10$ ** $p < .05$

initiative (i.e., to achieve direct modifying influence), they may in fact be able to block laws they oppose (i.e., to achieve direct preserving influence). I consider this possibility below.

I first assess the effect of opposition from different groups on a measure's success. As in tables 6.1 and 6.2, I consider the effects of financial contributions from economic interests, citizen interests, and a set of control variables on a measure's vote margin and probability of passage. These results are reported in table 6.5.

The second column of table 6.5 reports regression estimates relating vote margin to opposition spending by economic interests, citizen interests, whether the measure was an initiative, whether opponents waged a large ($1 million or more) campaign, and whether proponents waged a large ($1 million or more) campaign. I limit this analysis to measures that received some opposition spending from both economic and citizen interests.[12] The regression coefficients show that opposition spending by economic interests is associated with a lower vote margin, as expected. Opposition spending by citizen interests has no effect, and the vote margin is lower when the measure is an initiative and when there is a large campaign in favor of or against the measure.

The third column reports the logit estimates relating a measure's probability of passage to the same explanatory variables. We see that, as in the analysis of

[12] Results are similar but weaker when I include nine additional measures that received opposition spending from economic *or* citizen interests.

TABLE 6.6

Passage Rates of Initiatives with Majority and
Supermajority Opposition from Economic Interests
and Citizen Interests

Source of Opposition	Passage Rate (%)	
	50% Majority	*67% Majority*
Economic Professional Business	41 $N = 46$	40 $N = 42$
Citizen Occupational Individual	47 $N = 51$	50 $N = 44$

Sources: See table 5.8.

supporting contributions, the logit estimates are similar in sign and relative magnitude to the regression estimates but are weaker overall. Opposition spending by economic interests is associated with a lower probability of passage, although this effect is not statistically significant. Opposition spending by citizen interests has no overall effect.

I next compare the aggregate passage rates of measures that receive majority and supermajority opposition from economic and citizen interests. If economic interests are in fact better able to block initiatives through their opposition spending, I expect to see measures that receive majority and supermajority opposition from economic interests passing at a lower rate than measures that receive majority or supermajority opposition from citizen interests. These expectations are borne out in the data. Table 6.6 shows that 41 percent of initiatives that receive majority opposition from economic interests pass, whereas a higher share of initiatives that receive majority opposition from citizen interests—47 percent—pass. These differences are more stark for measures that received supermajority opposition from each group type: 40 percent of initiatives that receive supermajority opposition from economic interests pass, but 50 percent that receive supermajority opposition from citizen interests pass.

I then compare the sources of opposition spending for successful and unsuccessful initiatives. To the extent that economic interests are able to block initiatives through their opposition spending, I expect to observe unsuccessful initiatives receiving a large share of their opposition from economic interests and successful initiatives receiving a lower share of their opposition from economic interests. Table 6.7 reports the results of this analysis. As predicted, unsuccessful initiatives receive a greater share of their opposition from economic interests, although the difference between opposition from economic

TABLE 6.7
Sources of Opposition to Successful and
Unsuccessful Initiatives

Source of Opposition	Successful Initiatives (%)	Unsuccessful Initiatives (%)
Economic Professional Business	37	48
Citizen Occupational Individual	47	44
Other contributors	16	8
Total	100	100

Sources: See table 5.8.

and citizen interests is small. Successful initiatives receive a substantially lower share of their opposition from economic interests. Together, the analyses in tables 6.5–6.7 provide confirming evidence that economic interests are better able than citizen interests to use their monetary resources to block direct legislation measures they oppose.

Subject Areas and Passage Rates

My fourth set of analyses considers the extent that differences in interest group behavior translate into differences in the substantive areas of initiatives and referendums that pass and fail. Citizen and economic groups pursue different sorts of policies that reflect the interests of their members and constituents. Firms and economic actors join economic groups to promote their economic interests. As we saw in chapter 5, these groups pursue policies that reflect the economic interests of their members. Individuals join citizen groups to promote interests that may or may not be economic. Citizen groups therefore pursue policies that reflect the interests of their members. To the extent that ballot measures reflect the motivations and activities of the groups that use the process, I expect the initiatives and referendums that actually pass to reflect the substantive concerns of the individual members of citizen groups. I expect the laws that do not pass to reflect the substantive concerns of the corporate members of economic groups.

To test whether successful measures reflect citizen group interests and unsuccessful measures reflect economic group interests, I use the subject area categorizations of each of the 161 ballot measures reported in chapter 5. Recall

TABLE 6.8

Passage Rates of Initiatives and Referendums by Subject Area

Subject Area	Number	Passage Rate (%)
Veterans	3	100
Gambling/Morality	7	71
Government & Political Process	32	66
Education	14	64
Corrections	14	64
Health & Welfare	22	59
Civil Rights/Civil Liberties	7	57
Transportation	10	50
Environment	21	48
Revenue & Tax	17	47
Business & Labor Regulations	15	33
Total	162	100

that these subject areas include government and political process; revenue and taxation; business and labor regulation; health, welfare, and public housing; environment and land use; civil liberties and civil rights; education; transportation; corrections; veterans; and gambling and public morality. Because economic interests support initiatives and referendums mainly in the areas of transportation, revenue and taxation, business and labor regulation, and the environment, I expect these measures to pass at relatively low rates. Citizen interests tend to support initiatives and referendums mainly in the areas of government and political process, gambling and public morality, education, environment, and health and welfare; therefore, I expect these measures to pass at a higher rate.

Table 6.8 shows the passage rates for measures in each subject category. This table provides strong support for the theory. The lowest passage rates, as expected, are in the areas of business and labor regulation, revenue and taxation, environment, and transportation, which are the four areas most commonly pursued by economic interests. Passage rates in the areas most commonly pursued by citizen interests are among the highest, including gambling and public morality (71 percent), government and political process (66 percent), and education (64 percent). Several of the other areas with high passage rates are noneconomic issues (i.e., veterans, civil liberties and civil rights, and corrections) that received low support from both economic and citizen interests. Finally, the one ambiguous category is environment. Although all ten categories contain some measures that attract the support of

TABLE 6.9
Successful and Unsuccessful Initiatives and Referendums
by Subject Area

Subject Area	% of Successful	% of Unsuccessful
Government & Political Process	23	16
Gamblin/Morality	15	3
Health & Welfare	14	13
Corrections	11	6
Environment	11	16
Education	10	7
Revenue & Tax	9	13
Transportation	5	7
Business & Labor Regulations	5	15
Civil Rights/Civil Liberties	4	4
Veterans	3	0
Total	100	100
	N = 93	N = 69

economic interests and some that attract the support of citizen interests, most categories are dominated by one contributor type or the other. Environment, by contrast, contains numerous measures supported by each contributor type, and hence the category—and the measures within the category—draws support from both economic and citizen interests. This ambiguity is reflected by the passage rate of environmental measures, which is lower than the passage rate for other citizen interest categories and is higher than the passage rate for most of the other economic interest categories. Thus, the conclusion from table 6.8 is that in the areas clearly reflecting citizen interests, passage rates are relatively high; in the areas reflecting economic interests, passage rates are relatively low; and in the areas reflecting both citizen and economic interests, passage rates are in the middle range.

Table 6.9 reports how these passage rates translate into successful and unsuccessful initiatives and referendums. The second column of table 6.9 shows that 23 percent of successful initiatives and referendums dealt with government and political process issues; 15 percent dealt with gambling and public morality issues; 14 percent dealt with health and welfare, etc. The third column shows the percentage of unsuccessful measures from each subject area.

The results in table 6.9 are also consistent with the theory. The second column shows that the largest percentages of successful initiatives and referendums were in the categories of government and political process; gambling and public morality; health and welfare; corrections; and education. All of these categories were areas predominantly pursued by citizen interests (except corrections, which received few supporting contributions from either citizen or economic interests). Three of the areas of primary focus for economic interests—revenue and taxation; business and labor regulation; and transportation—account for lower percentages of all successful measures. Environment again falls between the other citizen and economic subject areas. Comparing the data in the two columns shows that the four areas where citizen groups tend to concentrate their resources (government and political process; gambling and public morality; health and welfare; and corrections) account for a higher percentage of successful measures than of unsuccessful ones. The three areas where economic interests concentrate their resources (revenue and taxation; business and labor regulation; and transportation) account for a higher percentage of unsuccessful measures.

Summary and Conclusions

This chapter explored the direct policy consequences of interest group involvement in the direct legislation process. Analyzing data on the patterns of campaign contributions from several types of interest groups showed that, to a large extent, direct legislation policy outcomes reflect the forms of influence that economic and citizen groups pursue and the actions they take. In particular, direct legislation outcomes show that economic groups find it very difficult to pass new initiatives, whereas citizen groups are much more successful at modifying policy through the direct legislation process. Economic groups are more successful at blocking measures through opposition spending.

First, I analyzed the relationship between contributions to direct legislation campaigns from different types of groups and the vote margin and probability of success of a measure. I found that contributions from economic groups, professional groups, and businesses are associated with a lower vote margin and probability of passage, whereas contributions from citizen groups, occupational groups, and autonomous individuals do not have a significant effect (either positive or negative) on vote margin and probability of passage.

Second, I compared the passage rates of initiatives and referendums that received majority and supermajority support from economic interests and from citizen interests. I found that initiatives that received majority support from citizen interests passed at a significantly higher rate than those that received majority support from economic interests. Measures that received supermajority support from citizen interests also passed at a higher rate than those that received supermajority support from economic interests.

Next, I analyzed the aggregate sources of support for the set of successful and unsuccessful initiatives. I found that the set of successful initiatives received a greater share of supporting contributions from citizen interests than from economic interests, whereas unsuccessful initiatives received a much larger share of supporting contributions from economic interests. Successful initiatives also received a larger share of supporting contributions from citizen interests than did unsuccessful initiatives, and unsuccessful initiatives received a larger share of supporting contributions from economic interests than did successful initiatives.

Third, I analyzed the effects of opposition spending on a measure's vote margin and probability of passage; majority and supermajority opposition from economic and citizen interests on passage rates; and the share of opposition spending from economic and citizen interests to successful and unsuccessful initiatives. I found that opposition spending by economic interests is associated with a lower vote margin and probability of passage. Measures that received majority and supermajority opposition from economic interests passed at a lower rate than measures that received substantial opposition from citizen interests. Successful initiatives received less opposition spending from economic interests, whereas unsuccessful initiatives received more.

Finally, I tested for differences in passage rates by subject area and in the substantive areas of successful and unsuccessful initiatives and referendums. I found that initiatives and referendums in the subject areas most often pursued by citizen interests passed at a higher rate than those in areas most often pursued by economic interests. I also found that the set of successful measures reflected citizen interests, and the set of unsuccessful measures reflected economic interests.

Together, these results suggest that the laws that pass by direct legislation largely reflect the interests of citizen groups. These results show that the fears of critics who believe economic interest groups dominate direct legislation outcomes are not supported.

As the theory suggests, however, direct modifying influence is neither the only nor necessarily the most important form of influence available to groups using the direct legislation process. The analysis shows that economic groups may be able to block initiative legislation they oppose. The theory also suggests that interest groups may achieve indirect influence by pressuring legislators in their state. In the following chapter, I explore the indirect policy consequences of interest group involvement in the direct legislation process.

7

Indirect Policy Consequences

MY THEORY of group choice suggests that groups may sometimes use direct legislation, not with the intention of directly passing new laws, but rather of indirectly influencing policy. In particular, interest groups may use direct legislation as a way of pressuring other actors to pass or block legislation on their behalf. To the extent that groups are able to use direct legislation to pressure other actors, I expect their behavior to have consequences for policy outcomes outside the direct legislation arena.

This chapter explores the consequences of interest groups' use of direct legislation on *state legislative policy* outcomes. Certainly, influencing the state legislative process is not the only form of indirect influence that interest groups involved in direct legislation may have. For example, through their use of initiatives and referendums, interest groups may also be able to affect the national policy agenda. Many observers argue that this occurred in the area of immigration reform when Congress considered and passed major immigration legislation in the wake of California's Proposition 187 in 1994. Groups may also be able to use initiatives and referendums in one state to affect policy in other states. For example, by placing issues on the political agenda in one state, interest groups provide policy advocates in other states with a model for policy change (Walker 1969). Observers argue that this very effect occurred when several states such as Massachusetts and Michigan passed tax limitation measures shortly after the passage of California's Proposition 13 in 1979 (Sears and Citrin 1985). Within their own state, interest groups may be able to use direct legislation to pressure the courts to reconsider earlier decisions on issues such as gay rights, term limits, campaign finance reform, or affirmative action. Finally, interest groups may even be able to influence candidate elections by linking their initiatives to candidate campaigns.[1]

Although these various indirect effects may be important, my primary focus is on the ability of interest groups to pressure their own state legislatures through their use of direct legislation. I highlight the effects of direct legislation on the state legislative process for several reasons. First, the statewide direct legislation process and the state legislative process are both ways of amending state statutes or constitutions. From an interest group's perspective,

---

[1] Many observers argue that Pete Wilson's successful re-election campaign for governor of California in 1994 was largely the result of his campaign's association with Proposition 187 (see Radwin 1996).

then, statewide direct legislation and the state legislative process represent two alternative mechanisms for pursuing a given set of policy interests at a given level of government. Second, pressuring legislators in their own state is one of the primary objectives reported by groups in my survey (see chap. 5). In fact, state legislators are often the most important targets of interest groups direct legislation strategies. Third, the state legislative process is an area where indirect effects may be especially important. State legislators depend heavily on interest groups operating within their state (Gray and Lowery 1996). State legislators may therefore respond more readily to interest group pressures than to pressures from other policy actors. For all of these reasons, I expect to observe important indirect effects of interest group involvement in the direct legislation process on the behavior of state legislators. To the extent that these indirect effects are apparent, they provide a background for assessing the indirect effects of interest groups direct legislation strategies on other policy actors as well.

State Policy Differences

My analysis in this chapter focuses on the effects of interest group involvement in the direct legislation process on state legislators. As with the analysis of direct effects, the problems of assessing whose interests are served by a given measure—either a direct legislation proposition or a traditional legislative bill—arise in the analysis of indirect effects. Assessing indirect policy consequences poses other thorny operational problems as well. The first problem has to do with isolating interest group influence on the behavior of state legislators. In the analysis of direct effects, interest groups were the primary policy actors. As I discussed in chapter 2, interest groups are responsible for all stages of the direct legislation process: They draft the measure; qualify it for the ballot; run campaigns for and against; provide substantial financial and nonfinancial support; and protect the measure from legislative amendment and judicial review, or coordinate efforts to overturn the measure. Therefore, when a measure passes or fails, we can attribute at least some responsibility (although perhaps not sole responsibility) for that outcome to interest groups.

In the analysis of indirect effects, the role of interest groups is much more difficult to isolate. The reason for this difficulty is that the links between interest group activities and policy outcomes are mediated by state legislators. As Kingdon (1989) argued, legislative behavior is the result of a complex interaction between numerous personal and institutional factors. Interest groups may play an important role in this process, but they are certainly neither the only forces pressuring legislators, nor are they necessarily the most important. The problem of isolating the indirect effects of interest group involvement in the direct legislation process is therefore analogous to isolating the effects of direct lobbying or campaign contributions on legislative behavior. As Smith

(1995) noted, the results of empirical studies of interest group influence in Congress are quite mixed, largely as a result of the complexity of the legislative process and the complex interaction of the many factors that affect legislative decision making.

My solution to this problem involves analyzing the aggregate effects of interest group involvement in the direct legislation process across many policy areas. The discussion above suggests that the effect of a particular activity by a particular interest group on a particular policy outcome may be small relative to other considerations and difficult to isolate empirically. Still, if interest group influence is important in some or all state legislative decisions, then we ought to observe evidence of those effects on the broad patterns of policy outcomes. I therefore begin my analysis by comparing policy outcomes in states with and without direct legislation. If economic interest groups are able to use direct legislation to pressure state legislators, we would expect at least a subset of policies passed in direct legislation states to reflect their interests more closely than policies passed in states where they lack the direct legislation option. If citizen interest groups are able to pressure state legislators through the direct legislation process, we would expect some policies passed in direct legislation states to reflect their interests more closely. Although this approach to assessing interest group influence is itself somewhat indirect, it provides preliminary evidence regarding the ability of groups to pressure state legislators and ultimately to influence state policy outcomes.[2]

Table 7.1 reports policy outcomes in several issue areas for initiative and noninitiative states. The policy areas include: several aspects of tax policy such as the percentage of states with a general sales tax, sales tax rate, percentage of states with a personal income tax, percentage of general fund revenues from the personal income tax, percentage of states with a corporate income tax, and percentage of general fund revenues from the corporate income tax;[3] average percentage of state total general expenditure on education, welfare, highways, hospitals, natural resources, health, corrections, and police;[4] percentage of states with mandatory no fault automobile insurance;[5] percentage of states with the death penalty;[6] percentage of states with "three strikes" legislation;[7]

---

[2] Of course, an absence of policy differences between direct legislation and non-direct legislation states is not in itself evidence that interest groups are unable to influence legislative policy. It may be that one type of interest group (say, economic) can influence one or more laws, and another type of interest group (say, citizen) can influence other laws in the same policy area, and that one set of laws cancels the aggregate effects of the others. Or, it may be that one type of interest group can influence policy through the state legislative process, but other interest groups can influence policy through direct legislation or another policy arena, and that these effects cancel each other. I consider this second possibility in my analysis of parental consent requirements and the death penalty, below.

[3] *Source*: U.S. Department of Commerce (1995). Revenue figures are for fiscal year 1994.

[4] *Source*: U.S. Department of Commerce (1995). Expenditure figures are for fiscal year 1994.

[5] *Source*: Council of State Governments (1996).

[6] *Source*: U.S. Department of Justice (1996).

[7] *Source*: Council of State Governments (1996).

TABLE 7.1

Mean State Policies and Difference in Means or Proportions Test, Selected Policy
Jurisdictions, Initiative and Noninitiative States

Policy	Initiative States	Noninitiative States	Test Statistic	Significance
Sales tax	.87	.93	.66	.51
Sales tax rate	.05	.05	.71	.48
Personal income tax	.74	.96	2.27	**.02**[a]
Personal income tax as % of revenues	.27	.31	.98	.33
Corporate income tax	.87	.96	1.21	.23
Corporate income tax as % of revenues	.06	.06	.53	.60
% Education spending	.35	.35	−.37	.71
% Welfare spending	.22	.25	1.37	.18
% Highway spending	.10	.09	−2.05	**.05**[a]
% Hospital spending	.03	.04	2.38	**.02**[a]
% Natural resources spending	.03	.02	−2.82	**.01**[a]
% Health spending	.04	.04	−1.01	.32
% Corrections spending	.03	.03	.75	.46
% Police spending	.01	.01	.34	.74
No-fault insurance	.44	.41	.20	.85
Death penalty	.78	.70	.63	.53
Three strikes	.35	.59	1.73	**.08**[a]
Lottery	.70	.74	.35	.72
Lottery revenues	558.30	509.15	−.24	.81
Parental consent	.83	.74	.73	.47
Abortion rate	.20	.21	.51	.61

[a] Bold-faced numerals indicate that the test statistic is significant at the .10 level.

percentage of states with a lottery program;[8] lottery revenues in millions of
dollars;[9] percentage of states requiring parental consent for teenage abortions;[10] and the abortion rate.[11] Because I am interested in the effects of interest groups on state legislative policy outcomes, I include in table 7.1 only
policies in areas in which the states have substantial jurisdiction. Clearly, however, this list of state policy areas is not exhaustive; states are involved in
numerous other policy areas not included in this analysis. Nor are the policy
areas in table 7.1 under the exclusive jurisdiction of the states. In all of these
areas, state governments share some responsibility with other government en-
tities such as local or federal governments. The included areas are, however,

[8] *Source*: U.S. Department of Commerce (1998).
[9] *Source*: U.S. Department of Commerce (1998).
[10] *Source*: NARAL Foundation (1998).
[11] *Source*: Henshaw and VanVort (1994). Number of abortions per 1,000 women.

some of the most important policy areas in which the states have primary jurisdiction.

The second column of table 7.1 reports the mean value of each policy (or the percentage of states with the policy) for initiative states and the third column reports the mean value for noninitiative states. The fourth and fifth columns of table 7.1 report the test statistic for a difference in means or proportions test and the level of significance for each of the selected policy areas.[12] The null hypothesis is that the means or proportions are equal (i.e., the presence of direct legislation has no effect on policy). In the area of tax policy, the only significant difference between initiative and noninitiative states is whether the state has an individual income tax. I find that although 96 percent of the noninitiative states tax personal income, only 74 percent of the initiative states do, and this difference is statistically significant at the .02 level. Once we account for whether states have a personal income tax, however, we find that the difference in the percentage of tax revenues from that source is not significantly different, on average, in initiative and noninitiative states, nor are other differences in tax policy.[13]

Table 7.1 also reveals some important differences in how initiative and noninitiative states spend their general revenues. Initiative states allocate a significantly greater share of their general expenditures to highway and natural resource spending and a significantly lower share to hospitals. Initiative states do not, however, spend significantly more or less on education, welfare, health, corrections, or police.[14] Note that highway and natural resource spending are policies in two of the subject areas where economic interest groups allocate the greatest shares of their direct legislation resources (i.e., transportation and environment). Note further, however, that only the difference in highway spending is more favorable to economic interest groups in initiative states (i.e., more spending). The percentage of spending on natural resources is also higher in initiative states. In this policy area, however, we would expect economic interests to prefer less, rather than more, spending. In fact, initiative states spend more on natural resources. Hospital spending is in one of the most important subject areas for citizen groups (health and welfare) and spending is higher in initiative states. These results thus suggest that, although citizen groups may be able to use direct legislation more effectively to influence policy directly,

---

[12] To test for differences in the percent of initiative versus noninitiative states with a given policy, I use a two-sample test of proportions. To test for differences in the average value of a policy in initiative versus noninitiative states, I use a two-sample t-test (assuming equal variances).

[13] In related work, Matsusaka (1995) compared taxes and spending in initiative and noninitiative states. In addition to the straight comparisons in policies across initiative and noninitiative states, Matsusaka controlled for other mediating factors such as state population characteristics and economic conditions. Although his argument regarding what brings about policy differences is different from the one posed here, his results are not inconsistent with my findings. He finds that total fiscal activity—both taxes and spending—is lower in initiative states than in noninitiative states.

[14] In several of these policy areas, average differences between initiative and noninitiative states are large, but so is variability within each category.

they are also able to influence policy indirectly in some subject areas. Economic groups, while much less effective in achieving direct influence, may also have some limited indirect influence.

The patterns reported in table 7.1 are consistent with the hypothesis that in some subject areas, interest groups can use direct legislation to pressure state legislators to pass laws that they would not otherwise. Two issues make inferences about the effects of interest groups activities problematic, however. The first problem is that the analyses do not isolate policies passed by the legislature from those passed by the initiative itself. Indeed, in most of the policy areas included in table 7.1, such as spending on environmental and public health policies, some of the relevant laws that determine current policy were passed by the state legislature, and some were passed by initiative. Therefore, we cannot determine how much of the differences in policy are the result of the legislature's response to interest groups' use of direct legislation or how much are caused by voters' passing initiative legislation themselves. In other words, the direct and indirect effects of interest group behavior are conflated. Second, the analyses in table 7.1 simply compare policies in initiative and noninitiative states. Without controlling for other causes of policy differences, it is impossible to isolate the effect of interest group use of the initiative.

In addition to these limitations, there is reason to expect that simply comparing policies across initiative and noninitiative states, even controlling for state population and economic characteristics, may produce misleading results. The model of interest group–legislator–voter interaction described in chapter 2 suggests that when groups pressure the legislature by threatening to propose an adverse initiative, we can expect a specific effect on policy. The model shows that when legislatures in initiative states respond to the threat of initiatives, they pass laws that are closer to both the interest group's most preferred policy and to the most preferred policy of the state's median voter than do legislatures in noninitiative states, if all else is constant. When legislators respond to interest group signals, they are likely to pass laws preferred by interest groups that lack majority voter support and hence that are further from the state's median voter. This implies that, to the extent that interest groups are able to achieve this form of indirect influence, there should not only be differences in policy outcomes in initiative versus noninitiative states, but there should also be differences in the relationship between policy, on the one hand, and voter and interest group preferences, on the other. Indeed, differences in policy outcomes alone could simply be the consequence of differences in voter preferences.

From the perspective of estimating the effects of interest group behavior on policy, the relationship between interest group and voter preferences turns out to be very useful. Interest group preferences are extremely difficult to estimate, especially independent of the strategies they adopt. Voter preferences, although also problematic in some ways, are much easier to estimate, especially with the use of survey data. Therefore, in light of these methodological issues, I further explore the indirect effects of interest group behavior by analyzing the

TABLE 7.2

Parental Consent Requirements and the Death Penalty, 1990

State	Consent/ Notice[a]	Death Penalty[b]	State	Consent/ Notice	Death Penalty
Ala.	Y/N	Y	Mont.	Y/N	Y
Alaska	Y/N	N	Nebr.	N/Y	Y
Ariz.	Y/N	Y	Nev.	N/Y	Y
Ark.	N/Y	Y	N.H.	N/N	Y
Calif.	Y/N	Y	N.J.	N/N	Y
Colo.	Y/N	Y	N.M.	Y/N	Y
Conn.	N/N	Y	N.Y.	N/N	N
Del.	Y/N	Y	N.C.	N/N	Y
Fla[c]	Y/N	Y	N.D.	Y/N	N
Ga.	N/Y	Y	Ohio	N/Y	Y
Hawaii	N/N	N	Okla.	N/N	Y
Idaho	N/Y	Y	Oreg.	N/N	Y
Ill.	Y/Y	Y	Pa.	Y/N	Y
Ind	Y/N	Y	R.I.	Y/N	N
Iowa	N/N	N	S.C.	Y/N	Y
Kans.	N/N	N	S.D.	Y/N	Y
Ky.	Y/N	Y	Tenn.	Y/N	Y
La.	Y/N	Y	Tex.	N/N	Y
Maine[c]	N/Y	N	Utah	N/Y	Y
Md.	N/Y	Y	Vt.	N/N	N
Mass.	Y/N	N	Va.	N/N	Y
Mich.[d]	N/N	N	Wash.	Y/N	Y
Minn.	N/Y	N	W.V.	N/Y	N
Miss.	Y/N	Y	Wis.	N/N	N
Mo.	Y/N	Y	Wyo.	Y/N	Y

Note: N, no; Y, yes.

[a] Includes both parental consent and parental notification requirements. *Source*: The NARAL Foundation, 1991, 1993.

[b] *Source*: Council of State Governments, 1992, pp. 549–51.

[c] Law was repealed by 1992.   [d] Law was added by 1992.

relationship between (estimated) median voter preferences and policy outcomes for two of the policies analyzed in table 7.1: parental consent requirements for teenage abortions and the death penalty. I selected these cases because of the availability of survey data required to estimate voter preferences toward each policy in the state and because state legislatures rather than voters themselves passed all or most of the relevant legislation. Table 7.2 shows parental consent requirements and death penalty provisions in the American states as of 1990.[15]

[15] I report policies as of 1990 because the relevant survey data were collected in 1990 and 1992. I describe the survey data and estimation procedures below.

A caveat of this analysis is that, as discussed above, I only expect interest group strategies to affect legislative behavior and outcomes under certain circumstances. Specifically, for an interest group to be able to pressure a legislature through the threat of an initiative, several conditions must be met. First, there must be mobilized interest groups that can credibly threaten to propose initiatives. Second, there must be majority-preferred initiatives that could be proposed. For an interest group to signal its preferences to the legislature effectively through its use of direct legislation, state legislators must be sufficiently vulnerable to require interest group resources, and interest groups with valuable resources must exist. In the cases described below, it is reasonable to assume that all of these conditions were met. After describing the empirical model implied by my hypotheses about the indirect effects of interest group behavior, I describe the procedures I use to estimate median voter preferences and then present the empirical results.

Empirical Model of Policy Differences

Conceptually, my test of indirect effects involves estimating the relationship between voter preferences and legislative policy outcomes on the one hand, and whether the state allows the initiative plus other control variables on the other hand. This relationship implies

$$|Policy_j - V_j| = \gamma_0 + \gamma_1 Initiative_j + \gamma_2 \mathbf{X}_j + u_j. \tag{1}$$

In equation (1), the distance (i.e., the absolute value of the difference) between policy (*Policy*) and the state's median voter's preference (*V*) is posited as a linear function of whether the state has the initiative process (*Initiative*) and a vector of control variables measuring aspects of the state's population and political environment (**X**). If interest groups are able to use direct legislation to pressure the legislature by threatening to propose majority-preferred initiatives that the legislature opposes, I expect the coefficient on *Initiative* to be negative (less distance between policy and preferences). If interest groups are able to use direct legislation to signal their preferences for nonmajority-preferred initiatives, I expect the coefficient on *Initiative* to be positive.

Although equation (1) captures the conceptual relationship of interest, there are several practical problems with estimating equation (1). Most important, because both of the policies I analyze are binary in the sense that the state either does or does not have the policy, it is quite possible that preferences and policy are measured on different metrics.[16] To avoid problems of inference

---

[16] The following example illustrates this scaling problem. Suppose the relevant policy data is binary, so that the endpoints naturally fall at 0 and 1 in the unidimensional policy space [0,1] with 0 indicating no policy and 1 indicating existence of the policy. Now suppose preferences are

resulting from preferences and policy being measured on different metrics, I express equation (1) as a logistic regression as follows,[17]

$$\ln\left[\frac{\Pr(Policy_j = 1)}{1 - \Pr(Policy_j = 1)}\right] = \beta_0 + \beta_1 V_j + \beta_2 V_j * Initiative_j + \beta_3 \mathbf{X}_j. \quad (2)$$

In equation (2), I specify the log-odds of a state having a parental consent law or the death penalty as a linear function of the state's median voter's preference (*V*); an interaction between the median voter's preference and a dummy variable indicating whether the state has the initiative (*V*Initiative*); and a vector of exogenous control variables (**X**). The logit specification allows me to avoid scaling preferences onto the same [0,1] range as policy and instead to estimate the relationship between the probability that a state has a parental consent (or death penalty) law and preferences for that law. The *V*Initiative* interaction indicates the extent to which the relationship between preferences and policy are closer in initiative states. Like-signed coefficients on *V* and *V*Initiative* therefore serve as support for the prediction that interest groups in initiative states can pressure the state legislature to pass laws that it prefers, so long as a majority of voters also prefers the law to the legislature's ideal policy. Opposite-signed coefficients on *V* and *V*Initiative* suggest that interest groups in initiative states can use direct legislation to signal effectively their support for nonmajority preferred initiatives.

The model in equation (2) provides a baseline for estimating the extent that groups in initiative states can pressure the legislature to pass different laws than it would otherwise. As the discussion of direct legislation institutions in chapter 3 suggests, however, not all direct legislation states are created equal. In some states such as California and Oregon, interest groups easily access the ballot and use the process often; in other states such as Wyoming, Illinois, and

---

distributed over the policy space [.2,1] because of systematic reporting or response bias (see Gerber and Jackson 1993) so that a strong preference for no policy (*Policy* = 0) actually falls at .2 rather than 0. To simplify the illustration, assume also that there is consensus in each state for the existing policy such that all voters in states with *Policy* = 1 report a strong preference for the policy (*V* = 1) and all voters in states with *Policy* = 0 report a strong preference for no policy. With the reporting bias, however, it appears that the voters in states with the policy are better represented because |*Policy* − *V*| = 0 for them, whereas |*Policy* − *V*|=.2 for voters in nonpolicy states. To tie the example back into the current analysis, if initiative states are systematically more likely to have some policies—for example, to have parental consent requirements (which they are)—then the reporting bias may also carry through to bias our inferences about the threat of initiatives. Furthermore, even in the absence of reporting bias, the distribution of the error term of equation (1) will not be multivariate normal.

[17] I manipulate equation (1) as follows. I first remove the absolute value from the dependent variable, then add *V* to both sides of the equation and multiply *V* times *Initiative*. I then express the relationship as a logistic regression. This logistic regression is no longer vulnerable to problems introduced by policy and preferences being measured in different metrics because the logit coefficients automatically take these differences into account.

Oklahoma, direct legislation is used rarely. I expect interest group influence to be greater in states with greater ease of ballot access. To capture differences in direct legislation institutions and their mediating effects on indirect influence, I further revise equation (2) by adding another term,

$$\ln\left[\frac{\Pr(Policy_j = 1)}{1 - \Pr(Policy_j = 1)}\right] = \beta_0 + \beta_1 V_j + \beta_2 V_j * Initiative_j$$
$$+ \beta_4 V_j * Initiative_j * Sig_j + \beta_3 \mathbf{X}_j. \qquad (3)$$

Interpretation of V and $V*Initiative$ are as above: Like-signed coefficients suggest that interest groups in initiative states can pressure legislatures to pass (majority-preferred) policies over and above whatever influence they have in noninitiative states. Opposite-signed coefficients suggest that interest groups can use direct legislation to signal their preferences for nonmajority preferred policies. Then $V*Initiative*Sig$ tells how this effect is modified by high barriers to ballot access (Sig is measured as a dummy variable scored one if the state's signature requirement is 10 percent or higher). I expect the coefficient on $V*Initiative*Sig$ to be of the opposite sign and smaller in magnitude than the coefficient on $V*Initiative$, showing that the effect of the initiative is less when the signature requirement is high. Interpretation of the other control variables remains unchanged.

Estimating State Median Voter Preferences

Estimating a state's median voter's preferences toward policy presents a challenging problem. Several approaches to estimating aggregate voter preferences are employed in the literature.[18] My approach avoids many of the problems associated with estimating state aggregate public opinion by employing a uniquely suited data set. The 1988–90–92 Pooled Senate Election studies include random samples of households in each of the fifty states (Miller et al. 1993). In addition to obtaining basic demographic and political information about the respondents, the survey also asked questions about their positions on several policy issues. In particular, respondents were asked whether they favored or opposed a state law that would require parental consent for a teenager

---

[18] One approach employs aggregate state characteristics such as aggregate vote returns (see especially Erikson and Wright 1993; Kenny and Morton 1993) or demographics (Matsusaka 1995) as proxies of aggregate ideology. The problem with this approach is that, in general, these aggregate characteristics measure policy preferences only indirectly. A second approach to estimating state aggregate voter preferences employs survey data. Surveys have the advantage of directly measuring (individual) policy preferences. Most available surveys lack an adequate sampling framework for drawing inferences about voters in different states, however. Attempts to address these data problems can be found in the empirical literature on representation (e.g., see Jackson 1989).

under eighteen to obtain an abortion and whether they favored or opposed the death penalty.[19] In addition, respondents were asked whether they had voted in previous elections.[20] I take the mean preference of self-reported voters in each state sample as my estimate of the state's median voter's preference for each issue.[21]

Naturally, there are problems with using the Senate Election Study surveys. Most important, state subsample sizes are rather small, ranging from 151 to 223. This problem is unfortunate but is less severe than with many comparable national surveys.

Logit Estimates

Table 7.3 reports the results of the logit analysis of equation (3) for policy and preferences toward parental consent. The dependent variable is whether the state has a parental consent or notification policy.[22] The estimated coefficients on V and $V*Initiative$ support the main hypothesis of the spatial model. The positive coefficient on V indicates that states with more support for parental consent are more likely to have such policies. The positive and significant coefficient on the preference-initiative interaction indicates an even greater probability of having the policy in states with high levels of support and the initiative process. In other words, policy in states that allow for initiatives more closely matches the state's median voter's preference than policy in non-initiative states, suggesting that interest groups in those states are able to pressure the state legislature by threatening to propose majority-preferred initiatives that the legislature opposes. Further, the negative coefficient on $V*Initiative*Sig$ indicates that this effect is lower in initiative states with high signature requirements.

I include several variables in the model to account for mediating factors that are expected to affect the relationship between voter preferences and policy.[23]

---

[19] Not all questions were asked in all years. The parental consent and death penalty questions were asked in 1990 and 1992.

[20] Seventy-two percent of respondents reported voting, compared with an estimated 57.4 percent of the total population that reported voting in the 1988 presidential election (U.S. Department of Commerce 1991). Some of this discrepancy may be due to an oversampling of voters in the survey and some may be due to respondent misreporting.

[21] Using the mean preference as an estimate of the median voter's preference requires a symmetric distribution of voters over the policy space.

[22] I combine consent and notification policies in this analysis because they are largely substitutes. In Gerber (1996), I ran a similar analysis for consent policies only and for consent and notification policies separately. In those analyses, I found roughly comparable effects.

[23] Several other variables were included in the models in alternative specifications. To measure legislator preferences, I included size of the legislature (lower house, upper house, total); existence of divided government (split party control of executive and legislature, split control of two legislative houses); and nature of partisan majority (size of majority party, match between legislative majority and estimated median voter party). To measure interest group preferences, I included

TABLE 7.3
Logit Coefficients for Parental Consent and Notification
Requirements

Variable	Coefficient	Standard Error	t-Statistic
Constant	6.56	6.24	1.05
V	7.06	6.07	1.16
V*Initiative	7.45	2.81	2.65
V*Initiative*Sig	−3.58	2.66	−1.35
Professional	−9.30	3.75	−2.48
Turnover	−12.48	5.63	−2.22
Psuedo R^2	.33		
N	50		

$* p < .10.$ $** p < .05.$

To capture institutional factors that may affect the legislature's responsiveness to interest group pressures, I include a measure of the degree of professionalization of the legislature, *Professional*, and the amount of turnover in the state legislature, *Turnover*.[24] The strong, negative, and significant coefficients on *Professional* and *Turnover* indicate that, controlling for the effects of the initiative process, states with more professionalized legislatures and more stable (less competitive) legislatures are less likely to require parental consent.

Because the coefficients reported in table 7.3 are logit coefficients and are therefore difficult to interpret, table 7.4 reports predicted probabilities of a state's adopting a parental consent requirement implied by the estimated coefficients. Probabilities are reported for several values of the independent variables, in the presence and in the absence of the initiative, and (in initiative states) with low and high signature requirements. For ease of interpretation, the control variables *Professional* and *Turnover* are set at typical values.[25]

Two points are evident from the probabilities reported in table 7.4. First, most initiative states are predicted to have parental consent laws. The only initiative states not expected to have parental consent requirements are those in which voter support for parental consent is weak and ballot access is diffi-

---

number (total registered lobbyists, number in particular issue area); and financial strength (total dollar contributions, total contributions per legislator, contributions from issue-area interest groups). The reported specifications represent the "best" specifications in terms of statistical significance and fit.

[24] *Professional* is Squire's (1992) professionalization index. *Turnover* is the percentage of new members in the state legislature's lower chamber between 1979 and 1989 (Council of State Governments 1991, p. 127).

[25] *Professional* is set at .302, which reflects a moderate but above-average level of professionalization. *Turnover* is set at .80, which also reflects a moderate but above-average level of turnover. These values facilitate interpretation of table 7.4.

TABLE 7.4

Predicted Probabilities of Adopting Consent Requirements

Independent Variables		Predicted Probabilities	
Median Voter's Preference[a]	Signature Requirement (%)	No Initiatives	Initiatives
L	5	.1136	.7449
M	5	.3253	.9780
H	5	.5197	.9958
L	10	.1136	.3250
M	10	.3253	.7894
H	10	.5197	.9291

[a] L signifies low levels of voter support, set at the sample minimum value (0.5034). M signifies medium voter support, set at the sample mean (0.6911). H signifies high voter support, set at the sample maximum value (0.8056).

cult (i.e., signature requirement is high). By contrast, noninitiative states are much less likely to have parental consent laws at all levels of voter preferences and interest group costs. Only noninitiative states with very favorable voter preferences are predicted to adopt parental consent laws. Second, having the initiative makes a huge difference. At all levels of voter preferences and interest group costs, initiative states are more likely to adopt a consent requirement than their noninitiative counterpart states. In all cases, except when voter support is weak and the signature requirement is high, the difference between initiative and noninitiative states is substantial.

Table 7.5 reports logit estimates of equation (3) for the death penalty. As in the analysis of parental consent policy, like-signed coefficients on V and $V*Initiative$ imply that policies in initiative states more closely reflect the median voter's preference than do policies in noninitiative states. Opposite-signed coefficients on V and $V*Initiative$ imply that policies in initiative states less closely reflect the median voter's preference. A coefficient on $V*Initiative*Sig$ that is the opposite sign of the coefficient on $V*Initiative$ implies that the effect of interest groups' indirect influence in initiative states is lower when the state has a high signature requirement.

The coefficients on V and $V*Initiative$ are both positive and significant. The coefficient on V is significant at the .10 level, but the coefficient on $V*Initiative$ is significant at the .05 level. These results provide evidence that is again consistent with the hypothesis that legislatures in initiative states respond to the threat of initiatives by passing laws that more closely reflect their state's median voter's preference. The effect of $V*Initiative*Sig$ is negative, as hypothesized, and is significant at the .12 level. In addition, the effect of *Professional* is again negative and significant, showing that states with a more professionalized legislature are less likely to have the death penalty. The

TABLE 7.5
Logit Coefficients for the Death Penalty

Variable	Coefficient	Standard Error	t-Statistic
Constant	−29.34	15.01	−1.96
V	35.05	19.43	1.80
V∗Initiative	11.01	5.30	2.08
V∗Initiative∗Sig	−5.93	3.81	−1.56
Professional	−30.19	12.77	−2.36
Divided89	−5.49	2.57	−2.14
%Black	1.17	.54	2.14
Crime	.0012	.0005	2.10
Psuedo R^2	.72		
N	50		

* $p < .10$.   ** $p < .05$.

estimated effect of turnover was small and insignificant and therefore is excluded from this analysis; whether the state had divided government in 1989 (*Divided89*), however, does (negatively) affect the probability of having the death penalty. In addition, I included two variables to capture the racial composition and crime rate in the state, *%Black* and *Crime*. Both of these variables show a positive relationship with the probability the state has the death penalty, and both are significant at the .05 level.

Table 7.6 reports predicted probabilities of states adopting the death penalty for several values of the independent variables.[26] As with parental consent requirements, noninitiative states are expected to have the death penalty only when voter support for the policy is very high. When voter support for capital punishment is lower (reported here at its mean and minimum values) but still substantially above .5, the model predicts that the state will not have the death penalty.[27] When voter support for the death penalty is strong, the state is virtually certain to have the policy, whereas with parental consent, the probability of having the policy in noninitiative states with maximal voter support is barely above .5. In other words, the probability of having the death penalty in states with the lowest level of support is lower, and probability in states with the highest level of support is higher, than the comparable probabilities of having a parental consent requirement.

The last column of table 7.6 shows that initiative states with low signature

[26] In table 7.6, the value of *Professional* is set at .302, *Divided89* is set at 1, *%Black* is set at 5 percent, and *Crime* is set at 5,072.9. As with table 7.4, these values are chosen to ease interpretation of table 7.6.

[27] Note that by our measure of voter preferences, the median voter in all states is estimated to prefer the death penalty (i.e., *V* is greater than .50).

TABLE 7.6
Predicted Probabilities of Adopting the Death Penalty

Independent Variables		Predicted Probabilities	
Median Voter's Preference[a]	Signature Requirement (%)	No Initiatives	Initiatives
L	5	.0012	.5155
M	5	.1265	.8292
H	5	.9453	.9561
L	10	.0012	.0262
M	10	.1265	.0514
H	10	.9453	.0978

[a] L signifies low levels of voter support, set at the sample minimum value (0.6201). M signifies medium voter support, set at the sample mean (0.7580). H signifies high voter support, set at the sample maximum value (0.8944).

requirements are expected to have the death penalty at all levels of voter support. When support is at its minimum value, the estimated probability of a state having the death penalty goes from virtually zero (.0012) in noninitiative states to .5155 in initiative states. When voter support is at its mean or maximum, the death penalty is virtually certain. In initiative states with high signature requirements, by contrast, groups find it almost impossible to pressure the legislature to pass a death penalty law. The probability of having the death penalty in an initiative state with a high signature requirement and the minimum level of voter support is only .0262, barely above the probability estimated for a noninitiative state with low voter support. Furthermore, the probability associated with higher levels of voter support is even lower in initiative states with a high signature requirement than in noninitiative states. Thus, when ballot access is difficult, the presence of the initiative leads legislatures to pass laws that are even more divergent from voter preferences than when there is no initiative process at all.

To summarize the empirical results of this section, compared to states without initiatives, those with initiatives tend to produce legislative policies that more closely reflect estimated state median voters' preferences toward parental consent and the death penalty. The strength of this relationship varies according to the signature requirement, as suggested by the spatial model. The results are independent of differences in other features of the state political environment such as turnover, divided government, and professsonalization of the legislature. Together, these analyses are consistent with the hypothesis that interest groups in initiative states can use direct legislation to pressure their state legislature to pass laws that both the group and the majority of voters prefer over the legislature's ideal policy.

Summary and Conclusions

This chapter explored the indirect policy consequences of interest group involvement in the direct legislation process. I found statistically significant differences in state environmental, transportation, public health, and tax policies in initiative and noninitiative states. In a more detailed multivariate analysis of abortion and death penalty policies, I further found that policies in initiative states more closely reflect voter preferences than do policies in noninitiative states, and that this effect is greatest when access to the direct legislation process is easiest. This finding is consistent with the hypothesis that interest groups can pressure the legislature through the threat of proposing initiatives when measures exist that both the group and a majority of voters prefer. In such a case, the legislature averts the initiative proposal by passing a law that is closer to the median voter's preference.

Together, the evidence from this chapter and the last suggest that policy outcomes reflect the motivations and activities of the interest groups that use the direct legislation process. Direct legislation outcomes reflect the interests of citizen groups that use direct legislation to achieve direct modifying influence. Legislative policy outcomes in initiative states reflect the interests of groups that use direct legislation to achieve indirect influence. In the next chapter, I return to my discussion of the populist paradox and assess the paradox in light of these empirical results.

8

The Populist Paradox: Reality or Illusion?

IN LIGHT OF THE theoretical and empirical results described in the preceding chapters, I now reassess the populist paradox. Recall that the populist paradox is the allegation that the direct legislation process has been transformed from a tool of broad-based citizen interests to a tool of narrow economic interests. Populist and Progressive reformers envisioned direct legislation as a way of circumventing the power of economic interest groups in state legislatures. Modern critics of direct legislation argue, however, that because of their superior financial resources, these very same sorts of economic interest groups are now virtually able to buy favorable initiatives and referendums at the expense of broader citizen-based interests. The ability of economic groups to use the process this way, the critics argue, undermines the promise of direct legislation.

Economic Group Limitations

The arguments developed in the preceding chapters provide a theoretical basis for rejecting the claim that economic interest groups buy policy outcomes in the sense of achieving direct modifying influence. There are important barriers that groups must overcome to pass new laws as initiatives and referendums. Many of these barriers put economic interest groups at a comparative disadvantage. In particular, economic groups typically lack the resources required to persuade a statewide electoral majority to support a new initiative or referendum. We should not expect economic interest groups to pursue direct modifying influence very often because doing so is extremely costly and is often substantially more costly than many other available options for influencing policy.

This is not to say that economic groups will never try to pass new laws by initiative. In most elections, economic groups place measures on the ballot that they hope will win. Although their measures nearly always fail, economic groups may continue to place their measures on the ballot for several reasons. For some groups, the expected benefit of passing a new law is sufficiently high to outweigh the low probability of passage. This motivation is especially important in states like California, for example, where it is extremely difficult to amend initiatives and referendums once they pass. In these states, restrictions on postelection legislative amendments mean that successful groups can lock in their direct legislation policy victories and ensure the benefits of their policy success long into the future.

For other economic interest groups, the group's unique circumstances make it difficult to pursue traditional legislative strategies. For example, an economic group may be engaged in a policy battle with another economic group that is well connected in the legislature, thereby making it difficult for the group to achieve its policy goals by more traditional means. The legislative impasse this competition creates has led insurance companies and trial lawyers, adversaries who each have considerable access to state legislatures, to turn to the initiative process in several states. Nonetheless, in all of these cases, we rarely expect economic interest groups to prevail at the ballot box; their ability to place measures on the ballot is far greater than their ability to achieve direct modifying influence by passing initiative legislation.

The empirical evidence provides further basis for rejecting the allegation that economic interest groups buy policy outcomes through the direct legislation process. When asked, economic groups often report that their intention is not to pass new laws by initiative. They report the importance of other motivations and pursue activities that are more consistent with preservation of the status quo or indirect forms of influence. In addition, the measures that economic groups support pass at a lower rate than those supported by citizen groups, and the set of policy outcomes that ultimately results from the direct legislation process tends not to reflect the substantive interests of economic groups.

Thus, it appears that the immediate concerns of critics who allege that economic interest groups control the direct legislation process are unfounded. Even though economic interest groups spend a lot of money in the direct legislation process, this does not serve as proof that they now dominate the process that was intended to circumvent their power. Because of their limited ability to mobilize resources and translate resources into policy success, economic interest groups are severely constrained in their ability to achieve direct modifying influence.

This is not to say, however, that economic groups are unable to influence policy through their use of direct legislation. Simply placing one's issues on the ballot and, hence, into the public debate, may produce benefits for economic interests. By raising public awareness and establishing a starting point for policy formation, economic interests may "win," even if the measures they support fail to gain an electoral majority on election day.

The theory and data suggest that economic groups may also be able to use their financial resources to wage opposition campaigns to block initiatives they oppose. Economic interest groups devote a much greater share of their financial resources to campaigns to oppose initiatives than to campaigns to support initiatives, and the measures they oppose fail at a high rate. Thus, although they may be limited in their ability to modify the status quo, economic interest groups may be more successful at preserving the status quo policy.

The theoretical and empirical analyses also suggest other ways that economic groups may be able to influence policy through the direct legislation process short of passing new laws by initiative. Most important, the direct legislation process gives groups a potentially powerful means for pressuring state legislators. The theoretical discussion showed that groups may influence state legislative policy through the direct legislation process in at least two ways. Groups that advocate majority-preferred initiatives may be able to pressure the legislature into preempting their (credible) initiative proposals and passing laws that they would not otherwise. Groups that lack majority voter support but have other resources valuable to state legislators may use direct legislation to signal their preferences to the legislature through costly effort. Because narrowly focused economic interest groups typically lack the electoral support for their measures to pose a credible threat to an initiative proposal but do tend to have resources that state legislators value (especially cash), we expect the second option to be most valuable for them. In other words, the direct legislation process provides economic groups that already have access to the legislative process with yet another means of pressuring state legislators.

The empirical evidence provides mixed support for the claim that economic interest groups can use direct legislation to augment their already considerable influence over the state legislative process. The surveys show that economic interest groups that use direct legislation report signaling the state legislature as their most important motivation for using the process. The analyses of policy outcomes in chapter 7 provide only limited evidence of their success, however. Comparison of policies in initiative and noninitiative states shows that, in most areas, differences in policy outcomes are not statistically significant when states have the initiative process and interest groups have that additional tool for influencing policy. The aggregate policy differences we do find are, in fact, in areas that are of importance to economic interest groups (i.e., transportation, environment, health and welfare, and revenue and taxation). In only one of these areas (transportation), however, are policies in initiative states more reflective of the interests of economic interest groups. In the other areas (revenue and taxation, health and welfare, and environment), policies in initiative states more closely reflect noneconomic citizen interests, suggesting that the first form of indirect influence (i.e., pressuring the legislature by credibly threatening to propose initiatives that the legislature opposes) dominates.

The in-depth analyses of differences in parental consent requirements and the death penalty further support the finding that citizen groups may be just as likely to achieve indirect influence as economic groups. In both of these policy areas, state legislative policy outcomes in initiative states more closely reflect the estimated preferences of the state's median voter. Thus, to the extent that interest groups can effectively pressure the state legislature, the evidence in these two areas is that groups whose own interests are consistent with broad-based citizen interests have been most effective.[1]

I conclude that the ability of economic interest groups to modify policy through the direct legislation process, either directly or even indirectly, is severely limited. Their main effect is to prevent new initiatives from passing. Hence, their influence over policy through the direct legislation process is largely conservative.

Citizen Group Dominance

Citizen groups have a comparative advantage at mobilizing the necessary resources to achieve direct modifying influence. Their problem is mobilizing other resources, especially money, to overcome barriers inherent in the drafting, qualifying, and campaigning phases of the direct legislation process. When they can mobilize monetary resources, citizen groups are better positioned than economic groups to mobilize an electoral majority and achieve direct modifying influence. This, of course, is largely as the Populists and Progressives planned.

The empirical evidence shows the importance of direct modifying influence for citizen interest groups. In their survey responses, citizen groups attribute greater importance to passing new laws by initiative than they do to all but one other motivation. Their patterns of contributions show that citizen groups dedicate more monetary resources to pursuing modifying influence than to pursuing preserving influence, and they dedicate more monetary resources to pursuing modifying influence than do economic groups. Finally, aggregate outcomes show that citizen groups are more successful than economic groups at actually passing new laws by initiative. Initiatives supported by citizen groups pass at a higher rate than those supported by economic groups, and the set of successful initiatives reflects citizen group support and substantive interests.

Implications for the Study of Direct Legislation

These results have important implications for future studies of direct legislation. Perhaps the most significant such implication is the importance of understanding the numerous forms of influence that groups can have. Groups use

[1] Of course, these two policies are not a random sample of all possible policy areas in which groups may have indirect influence. Rather, they were chosen because of the availability of survey data and because state legislatures were responsible for all or most of the relevant legislation. Still, in combination with the aggregate comparisons of policy differences in initiative and noninitiative states, these analyses illustrate the potential importance of interest group pressure through the direct legislation process.

direct legislation to pass new laws, to block legislation they oppose, and to pressure state legislators. To the extent that previous work on direct legislation has considered policy consequences, it has focused almost exclusively on direct policy consequences. My research illustrates, however, that new initiative laws are only one of the possible policy consequences of the direct legislation process, and in many policy areas, they may not even be the most important consequence. Assessing only the direct policy consequences of interest group involvement in the direct legislation process therefore risks seriously underestimating the full extent of their influence over policy outcomes.

A related implication is the importance of understanding interest group motivations. Interest groups use direct legislation for a variety of reasons. Groups sometimes use direct legislation because they believe their chances of qualifying and passing new initiatives are high; other times, they use direct legislation because their prospects for policy success in the legislative process is very low; at still other times, they use direct legislation for nonpolicy reasons such as appeasing member demands, developing networks, and drawing attention to their group and its agenda. Furthermore, these differences are not random; they are intimately related to the resource constraints groups face. Studies of the direct legislation process that seek to understand how and why interest groups use the direct legislation process must therefore recognize the multiplicity of group motivations for using direct legislation. Studies that attempt to assess a group's success must do so in terms of its ability to meet its objectives.

Implications for the Study of Interest Group Influence

As I mentioned in chapter 1, much of the motivation for this study results from my desire to inform the study of interest group influence more generally. One lesson from this study is that groups often have numerous ways of pursuing their policy goals. Most studies of interest group influence focus on only a small subset of interest group activities. My research shows that we must understand those activities as the result of a strategic choice in which groups weigh the expected costs and benefits of alternative activities. I am not arguing that all interest groups necessarily assess each and every policy alternative available to them and maximize their expected net benefit in a strict economic sense. Rather, groups face choices, and what we observe regarding interest group activities is often a glimpse of the political process that follows a group's decisions about how to pursue its policy goals.

Groups also choose which forms of influence to pursue. My research implies that interest groups in all policy arenas may pursue many different forms of influence, and to focus on only one or a few may risk seriously underestimating their overall impact on policy. Most important, we must recognize not only a group's ability to alter policy but also its ability to block policy changes and to influence other political actors.

My study also emphasizes the importance of group resources. Resources allow a group to overcome the barriers to influence inherent in all policy processes. Recognizing how resources constrain what a group can and cannot do is therefore important both in terms of understanding a group's decisions about how to pursue policy and assessing a group's success in achieving its goals.

Positive versus Normative Implications

Finally, it is important to address the normative implications of my research. Throughout this book, I have focused exclusively on the positive or descriptive aspects of interest group involvement in the direct legislation process. I have tried hard not to attach normative value to any particular set of outcomes or to any particular balance of interest group power. I have tried only to describe the set of policies that result from interest group use of direct legislation and the relative power of the actual groups that use the process. No doubt, however, some readers will attribute normative meaning to the conclusions I draw. To many, the conclusion that citizen groups are able to use direct legislation to pass new laws will be interpreted as good, as will the conclusion that economic groups are unable to do so. This, however, is not the point of this book, nor is it a necessary implication of my results. To close, it is important to be clear about what I take to be the normative implications raised by my analysis.

I do *not* say that citizen group dominance of the direct legislation process is necessarily good. The normative value one attributes to this finding depends very strongly on one's assessment of whether majoritarian interests already receive sufficient representation in modern American government. Certainly, the early Populist and Progressive advocates of direct legislation took the position that minority interests, especially those of certain powerful industries, were overrepresented in state legislatures at the expense of broader middle-class interests. To the extent that one agrees that those same sorts of narrow economic interests are overrepresented in state legislatures today, the normative implication of citizen group dominance is favorable. In contrast, to those who believe that business or economic interests are limited in their ability to influence state legislatures or that they hold appropriate levels of power in the state legislative process, the shift of power toward majoritarian interests may be interpreted as bad. Most important, to those who believe the state legislative process facilitates compromise between competing interests, empowering the majority through the direct legislation process threatens to upset the delicate balance between majority and minority interests.

Regardless of whether one believes minority interests are overrepresented, trade-offs come with empowering majoritarian interests through the direct legislation process. First, empowering the state's majority through direct legislation may result in disregard for basic minority rights. As Madison argued, "measures are too often decided, not according to the rules of justice and the rights of the minor party, but by the superior force of an interested and over-bearing majority" (Madison in Hamilton et al. 1961, p. 77). In the legislative process, minority interests have multiple points of access and consequently have multiple points at which they can pursue their interests. In direct legis-lation, minorities lack the same abilities to promote their interests. Laws are made directly by the voting majority, while minority interests (i.e., any interests that receive less than majority support) are excluded from the policy-making process. In other words, direct legislation lacks the checks and bal-ances that provide minority groups with multiple points of access in the legis-lative process. As a result, minority interests have no real recourse against an overbearing majority, short of blocking direct legislation measures entirely or challenging initiative and referendum legislation in the courts.

The dominance of citizen interest groups in the direct legislation process exacerbates the problem of protecting minority interests. Citizen groups often mobilize around social and moral issues that have clear winners and losers. For the minority interests that cannot mobilize an electoral majority, the conse-quences of a direct legislation policy may be severe. Unless they are able to create sufficient opposition to block the initiative or referendum, the state and federal courts represent their last and only resort.

A second important trade-off is related to the problem of redistribution. In direct legislation, the people who vote on and benefit from initiatives and refer-endums do not necessarily share the preferences of the people who do not vote and, hence, are denied benefits (Schrag 1998). Compared to the overall popula-tion, voters in direct legislation elections tend to be wealthier, better educated, older, more conservative, and are more likely to be white (Magleby 1984). Many of the measures these voters pass, particularly tax reform measures, reflect their privileged socioeconomic positions (Hahn and Kamieniecki 1987). For example, voters in several states have passed initiatives that limit the state's ability to raise property taxes. These tax limitations have had nu-merous consequences. Most important, they have meant that revenues must be made up from other sources, shifting the tax burden from increasingly elderly property owners to others in the state (Sears and Citrin 1985). In addition, property tax limitations have reduced the flow of revenues into states' general funds. As a result, the policies financed by the general fund, especially redis-tributive policies, are under pressure, while earmarked spending programs such as entitlements remain protected.

Although the net results of initiative policies on the redistribution of a state's wealth are not fully understood, it is clear from the tax limitation exam-ple that the direct legislation process provides voters with a means of altering the distribution of power and wealth in favor of those who vote and against those who do not.

In addition to the question of citizen group dominance is the question of economic group limitations. My positive analysis showed that economic groups play a largely conservative role in the direct legislation process by blocking initiatives they oppose. What are the normative implications of this conservative influence of economic groups?

To advocates of direct legislation, the fact that economic groups can prevent citizen groups and others from using the process to pass new laws may be viewed as a weakening of an important tool for majoritarian interests. As a result of collective action and coordination problems, it may be very difficult for broad-based citizen interests to organize and achieve legislative success. The problems faced by majoritarian interests may be especially severe when there is a well-organized minority that can effectively oppose their interests in the state legislature. Proponents of direct legislation argue that it represents an important alternative to the state legislative process that majoritarian interests often find so difficult to access. Weakening this tool therefore means weakening the one real means by which broad-based citizen interests can hope to offset the advantage of economic interests.

Similarly, proponents of direct legislation argue that economic groups already have substantial power in the legislature. The conservative influence they gain through direct legislation only means that economic interest groups have even more power to protect the policy gains they achieve in the statehouse.

To critics of the direct legislation process, the conservative influence of economic interest groups may be of little concern. Indeed, some would argue that, because of the other problems associated with most successful initiatives and referendums, the ability of economic groups to protect against the mischief of users of direct legislation may be a good thing. Most important, many observers argue that citizens are not competent to decide complex public policy issues (California Commission on Campaign Financing 1992). To them, the conservative influence of economic interest groups protects citizens from the potential harm done by their very inability to comprehend fully and evaluate initiative and referendum legislation.

Critics of direct legislation who claim that citizens are not competent to decide complex public policy issues often point to the lack of substantive information most voters have about the initiatives and referendums they decide. Magleby (1984) reported that voters have low levels of interest in and information about statewide ballot propositions. This is especially true among the least-educated segments of the population. Cronin (1989, p. 87) added, however, that direct legislation voters are "not as competent as we would like them to be, yet not as ill informed or irrational as critics often insist."

Others argue that steps must be taken to make initiatives easier to understand. The California Commission on Campaign Financing (1992) report urged limiting initiatives to five thousand words, requiring meaningful public hearings, expanding disclosure requirements, improving the ballot pamphlet, and providing new information services. Dubois and Feeney (1992) made similar recommendations, such as limiting the number of initiatives, providing better information about competing initiatives, requiring legislative preelection review, enforcing the single-subject law, improving the ballot pamphlet, and expanding disclosure requirements. Although they do not explicitly claim that voters are poorly informed and/or ill equipped to decide complex policy issues under the current direct legislation provisions, all of these recommendations imply that the process will be improved by reducing complexity and voter uncertainty.

Still, the question of voter competence remains open to debate. A lack of substantive information or the presence of a complex policy issue does not mean that voters cannot make good decisions. Theoretical and empirical research by Lupia (1994) and Gerber and Lupia (1995, 1998) showed the conditions under which voters can make good decisions. Lupia (1994) found that when voters could identify the positions of sponsors of the five California insurance initiatives in 1988, they were able to identify which of the several propositions were in their economic self-interest. Gerber and Lupia (1995, 1998) also showed that when initiative and referendum campaigns are competitive, providing campaign messages from both sides of an issue, voters are better able to cast "informed votes" similar to those they would have cast if they had more information. In Bowler and Donovan's (1998) study, voters were able to make reasonable decisions in direct legislation elections across a range of issues. Together, these works suggest that, even though initiatives may be complex and confusing and voters may lack detailed substantive information about the measures, they may still be competent to choose between the electoral alternatives.

Related to the question of citizen competence is the question of unintended consequences. Critics charge that, although any law may have unintended consequences, those passed by initiative and referendum may be harder to amend, thereby making those consequences more difficult to correct. In addition, critics contend that because the direct legislation drafting process lacks many of the procedures that allow input from diverse interests and experts, the laws that result may contain more unintended consequences in the first place.

The problem of unintended consequences means that voters may not be able to anticipate the longer-run implications of their choices even if they are competent to figure out which policy alternative is more consistent with their preferences *at face value*. Thus, they may vote for one policy and effectively receive another. To the extent that the ultimate consequences of initiatives and referendums, both intended and unintended, diverge from some measure of citizen interests, the fact that economic groups can prevent these laws from being adopted may be viewed with less concern.

A Final Assessment

In light of these positive and normative issues, what can be said about the ability of economic interest groups to use direct legislation at the expense of broader citizen interests? Is the populist paradox, in fact, a paradox?

Certainly, the role and influence of economic interest groups is different from what modern critics charge. Economic groups are limited in their ability to achieve direct influence over policy, especially direct modifying influence. At the same time, however, direct legislation provides them with additional means for influencing policy in more subtle ways. In terms of ultimately influencing policy, these additional means may be every bit as important as passing new laws by initiative. To the extent that economic interests are able to influence policy through the legislative process, direct legislation provides them with an important mechanism for enhancing and protecting their legislative advances. Thus, although the influence of economic interest groups over policy may be conservative or indirect, it is contrary to the intentions of the Populist and Progressive reformers.

Appendix A

Direct Legislation Institutions

TABLE A.1
Direct Legislation Provisions, 1996

State	Direct Legislation Provision[a]	State	Direct Legislation Provision[a]
Ala.	—	Mont.	DI, PR
Alaska	II, PR	Nebr.	DI, PR
Ariz.	DI, PR	Nev.	DI, II, PR
Ark.	DI, PR	N.H.	—
Calif.	DI, PR	N.J.	—
Colo.	DI, PR	N.M.	PR
Conn.	—	N.Y.	—
Del.	—	N.C.	—
Fla.	DI	N.D.	DI, PR
Ga.	—	Ohio	DI, II, PR
Hawaii	—	Okla.	DI, PR
Idaho	DI, PR	Oreg.	DI, PR
Ill.	DI	Pa.	—
Ind.	—	R.I.	—
Iowa	—	S.C.	—
Kans.	—	S.D.	DI, PR
Ky.	PR	Tenn.	—
La.	—	Tex.	—
Maine	II, PR	Utah	DI, II, PR
Md.	PR	Vt.	—
Mass.	II, PR	Va.	—
Mich.	DI, II, PR	Wash.	DI, II, PR
Minn.	—	W.Va.	—
Miss.[b]	II	Wis.	—
Mo.	DI, PR	Wyo.	II, PR

Source: Dubois and Feeney 1992, State Election Officials.

[a] DI, Direct Initiative; II, Indirect Initiative; PR, Popular Referendum.

[b] Mississippi adopted a form of indirect initiatives in 1992. However, since the process did not actually result in a qualified ballot measure until after the period considered in my study, I categorize Mississippi as a non-direct legislation state.

TABLE A.2
Drafting Stage Institutions

State	Single Subject Law[a]	Content Restrictions[b]	Preelection Review[c]
Alaska	Y	Y	A
Ariz.	Y	N	—
Ark.	N	N	A, J
Calif.	Y	N	L
Colo.	Y	N	A
Fla.	Y	N	J
Idaho	Y	N	A
Ill.	Y	N	—
Maine	N	N	—
Mass.	Y	Y	A
Mich.	Y	N	—
Miss.	N	Y	A
Mo.	Y	Y	J
Mont.	Y	Y	A, J
Nebr.	Y	Y	A, J
Nev.	Y	Y	—
N.D.	Y	N	—
Ohio	Y	Y	—
Okla.	Y	N	—
Oreg.	Y	N	A
S.D.	N	N	—
Utah	Y	N	J
Wash.	Y	N	A
Wyo.	Y	Y	—

Source: Dubois and Feeney 1992, State Election Officials.

[a] In most states, single subject requirements apply to all types of direct legislation (direct initiatives, indirect initiatives, statutory measures, constitutional amendments) that the state allows. Five states that allow both statutes and constitutional amendments restrict content to a single subject for one type but not the other (Michigan, Nevada, Arizona, Colorado, North Dakota). Some state requirements are ambiguous.

[b] Includes prohibitions on taxation and appropriations, special or local legislation, changes in jurisdiction of the courts, changes in the amendment process, and changes affecting freedom of speech, press, elections, assembly, just compensation, or right of access to courts.

[c] A = administrative. Includes provisions for administrative review of constitutionality. Nineteen states require election officials to review propositions for format and language. J = judicial. Includes provisions for preelection judicial review of constitutionality. L = legislative.

TABLE A.3
Qualifying Stage

| State | Signature Requirement | | Popular Referendum |
	Statutory	Constitutional	
Alaska	10	—	10
Ariz.	10	15	5
Ark.	8	10	6
Calif.	5	8	5
Colo.	5	5	5
Fla.	—	8	—
Idaho	10	—	10
Ill.	—	8	10
Ky.	—	—	5
Maine	10	—	10
Md.	—	—	3
Mass.[a]	3 + .5	3	2
Mich.	8	10	5
Miss.	—	12	—
Mo.	5	8	5
Mont.	5	10	5
Nebr.	7	10	5
Nev.	10	10	10
N.M.	—	—	10
N.D.[b]	2	4	2
Ohio	3 + 3	10	6
Okla.	8	15	5
Oreg.	6	8	4
S.D.	6	8	5
Utah	5 + 5	—	10
Wash.	8	—	4
Wyo.	15	—	15

Source: Dubois and Feeney 1992, State Election Officials.

[a] First figure is percent to qualify indirect initiative; second is additional signatures to place measure on the ballot.

[b] Percent of resident population.

TABLE A.4
Campaign Stage

State	Committees Register	Committees Disclosure[a]	Individuals Disclosure	Sponsors Identify
Alaska	N	100	250	Y
Ariz.	N	25/all	—	Y
Ark.	Y	250	250	Y
Calif.	Y	100	500	Y
Colo.	Y	25	100	Y
Fla.	Y	all	50	Y
Idaho	Y	50/25	100	N
Ill.	Y	150	—	N
Maine	Y	50/all	50	Y
Mass.	Y	50/25	—	Y
Mich.	Y	20/50	100	Y
Miss.	Y	200	200	N
Mo.	Y	100	500	Y
Mont.	Y	75/all	—	Y
Nebr.	Y	100	100	Y
Nev.	N	—	—	N
N.D.	N	100	—	N
Ohio	Y	all	—	Y
Okla.	Y	200	—	Y
Oreg.	Y	100/all	100	Y
S.D.	N	100	—	Y
Utah	Y	50/all	—	Y
Wash.	Y	25/50	100	Y
Wyo.	Y	all	—	Y

Source: Dubois and Feeney 1992, State Election Officials.
[a] First figure refers to contributions; second figure refers to expenditures.

TABLE A.5
Postelection Stage

State	No Restrictions	Waiting Period	Supermajority Requirement
Alaska	—	2 years	—
Ariz.[a]	—	—	—
Ark.	—	—	⅔ vote
Calif.[a]	—	—	—
Colo.	Y	—	—
Fla.	—	—	—
Idaho	Y	—	—
Ill.	—	—	—
Maine	Y	—	—
Mass.	Y	—	—
Mich.	—	—	¾ vote
Miss.	—	—	—
Mo.	Y	—	—
Mont.	Y	—	—
Nebr.	Y	—	—
Nev.	—	3 years	—
N.D.	—	7 years	—
Ohio	Y	—	—
Okla.	Y	—	—
Oreg.	Y	—	—
S.D.	Y	—	—
Utah	Y	—	—
Wash.[b]	—	2 years	⅔ vote
Wyo.	—	2 years	—

Source: Dubois and Feeney 1992, State Election Officials.

[a] Requires vote of the people.

[b] Two-year waiting period OR two-thirds legislative vote.

University of California, San Diego
Department of Political Science
Survey of Organizations

This survey is part of a study of organizations and their participation in the direct legislation process. It is being conducted for academic purposes only and is not for profit or commercial use. Your organization was randomly selected for inclusion in our study from a list of several thousand organizations in eight states. The entire survey should only take about 15 or 20 minutes to complete. Please answer the following questions to the best of your ability and thank you for your participation.

Please verify the name and address of your organization and make the appropriate corrections where necessary.

_____   Corrections:

_____   Name: _____

_____   Address: _____

_____   _____

Your name: _____

Phone number: _____

Job Title: _____

The following is a series of questions about your organization's participation in the direct legislation process within the last five years. By direct legislation we mean both initiatives, which are propositions placed on the ballot by groups of citizens and then voted on, and referendums, which are submitted by the state legislature and placed on the ballot. These include both statutory measures and constitutional amendments.

1) Please indicate the number of times your organization has supported or opposed a statewide initiative or referendum by engaging in each of the following activities in the last **five** years.

   A. Publicly endorsed or opposed an initiative or referendum.

       0 (Never)   1   2–3   4–10   11+

   B. Provided information to or lobbied your members about an initiative or referendum.

       0 (Never)   1   2–3   4–10   11+

   C. Organized your members to circulate petitions for the purpose of qualifying an initiative.

       0 (Never)   1   2–3   4–10   11+

D. Shared your membership or mailing lists with organizations actively involved in an initiative or referendum campaign.

0 (Never)   1   2–3   4–10   11+

E. Made a nonfinancial contribution such as donating staff time or resources to an initiative or referendum campaign.

0 (Never)   1   2–3   4–10   11+

F. Made a financial contribution to an initiative or referendum campaign.

0 (Never)   1   2–3   4–10   11+

G. Sponsored fundraising activities to support an initiative or referendum campaign.

0 (Never)   1   2–3   4–10   11+

H. Joined a ballot measure committee that was formed to support or oppose an initiative or referendum.

0 (Never)   1   2–3   4–10   11+

I. Created a ballot measure committee to support or oppose an initiative or referendum.

0 (Never)   1   2–3   4–10   11+

J. Drafted initiative legislation to be placed on a statewide ballot.

0 (Never)   1   2–3   4–10   11+

K. Lobbied the state legislature to place a referendum on the ballot.

0 (Never)   1   2–3   4–10   11+

L. Other activities involving statewide initiatives or referendums.
Please specify. _____

0 (Never)   1   2–3   4–10   11+

2) Involvement in direct legislation includes any of the activities addressed in the previous question (from endorsements to financial contributions to drafting an initiative). With this in mind, how many separate initiative or referendum measures has your organization been involved with in the last **five** years? _____

3) In addition to using the initiative and referendum, there are many other ways in which an organization might act politically on behalf of its constituents and members. Following is a list of possible ways in which this can be done. Please indicate by check mark any other political activities your organization engages in.

__ A. Contribute to campaigns for candidates to a state legislature.

__ B. Contribute to campaigns for candidates to other state offices.

__ C. Contribute to campaigns for candidates to the U.S. Congress.

__ D. Coordinate letter writing, E-mail or telephone campaigns to inform state legislators of member policy positions.

__ E. Testify before a state government commission, hearing, or other legislative session.

__ F. Testify before a federal government commission, hearing or other legislative session.

___ G. Employ a lobbyist to represent your organization's interests in the state legislature.

___ H. Employ a lobbyist to represent your organization's interests in the U.S. Congress.

___ I. Work with state government agencies in policy formation and implementation (i.e., write comments or policy positions, or draft regulations).

___ J. Work with federal government agencies in policy formation and implementation.

___ K. Pursue issues through litigation in the courts.

___ L. Organize protests.

___ M. Seek to influence public opinion through the use of the mass media.

___ N. Other (please specify). _____

4) Which activities indicated by A through N in question 3 are most important to your organization? Please list up to three. _____ _____ _____

5) The direct legislation process is most often utilized to change **state policy or laws**. Given this limited scope, we would like to know what areas of **state policy** formation your organization is actively involved in. Please check all that apply.

___ A. Government structure or reform of political or electoral processes

___ B. Revenue and taxation

___ C. Business regulation or commerce

___ D. Labor regulation or workplace safety

___ E. Health-care policy

___ F. Welfare, public housing, or human services

___ G. Public morality (i.e., gambling, pornography)

___ H. Environmental policy

___ I. Agricultural policy

___ J. Civil rights/civil liberties

___ K. Education policy

___ L. Transportation policy

___ M. Penal code or criminal law

___ N. Other (please specify). _____

6) What is your organization's **main** area of state political activity? Please choose only one from the above list. _____

7) Has direct legislation been an effective way of pursuing your organization's political objectives **in the past**?   Yes ____   No ____

8) Would you consider using direct legislation to pursue your organization's political objectives **in the future**?   Yes _____   No _____

IF YOUR ORGANIZATION **HAS USED** DIRECT LEGISLATION IN THE PAST FIVE YEARS, PLEASE PROCEED TO QUESTION 9 BELOW. IF YOUR ORGANIZATION **HAS NOT USED** DIRECT LEGISLATION IN THE PAST FIVE YEARS, PLEASE SKIP QUESTIONS 9 AND 10 AND PROCEED TO QUESTION 11.

9) Each of the following is a possible objective that organizations might seek to accomplish through the use of direct legislation. Please indicate how important each objective was in your organization's decision to use direct legislation. (Complete this question only if your organization has used direct legislation in the past five years.)

Scale: 1 = not at all important to 5 = very important

	Not At All			Very
A. Passing desired legislation by initiative or referendum	1 2 3 4 5
B. Sending a signal to the state legislature about popular support for an issue	1 2 3 4 5
C. Pressuring the state legislature to place a new issue on its legislative agenda	1 2 3 4 5
D. Pressuring the state legislature to pass desired legislation	1 2 3 4 5
E. Drawing public attention to your organization	1 2 3 4 5
F. Drawing public attention to your organization's political agenda	1 2 3 4 5
G. Protecting legislation from amendments by the legislature	1 2 3 4 5
H. Complying with constitutional requirements	1 2 3 4 5
I. Responding to member demands for action	1 2 3 4 5
J. Developing networks with other organizations	1 2 3 4 5
K. Other _____	1 2 3 4 5

10) Please indicate the importance each of the following factors played when your organization decided to use direct legislation to pursue its objectives.

Scale: 1 = not at all important to 5 = very important

	Not At All			Very
A. Familiarity with the direct legislation process	1 2 3 4 5
B. High probability of qualifying an initiative	1 2 3 4 5
C. High probability of passing an initiative or referendum	1 2 3 4 5
D. Difficulty of using the legislative process (i.e., state legislature)	1 2 3 4 5
E. Previous experience with direct legislation	1 2 3 4 5
F. Availability of consultants	1 2 3 4 5

G. Support from members   1 2 3 4 5

H. Availability of resources   1 2 3 4 5

I. Availability of volunteers   1 2 3 4 5

PLEASE PROCEED TO QUESTION 12

IF YOUR ORGANIZATION HAS NOT USED DIRECT LEGISLATION IN THE PAST FIVE YEARS, PLEASE ANSWER QUESTION 11 BELOW

11) Please indicate the importance each of the following factors played in your organization's decision **not** to use direct legislation.

Scale: 1 = not at all important to 5 = very important

	Not At All				Very
A. Never considered using direct legislation	1	2	3	4	5
B. Lack of familiarity with the direct legislation process	1	2	3	4	5
C. Low probability of qualifying an initiative or referendum	1	2	3	4	5
D. High cost of qualifying an initiative or referendum	1	2	3	4	5
E. Low probability of passing an initiative or referendum	1	2	3	4	5
F. High cost of a direct legislation campaign	1	2	3	4	5
G. Wouldn't generate enough publicity	1	2	3	4	5
H. Wouldn't influence the legislature's behavior	1	2	3	4	5
I. Ease of using the legislative process (i.e., state legislature)	1	2	3	4	5
J. Resistance from members	1	2	3	4	5
K. Lack of volunteers	1	2	3	4	5
L. Stringent reporting requirements	1	2	3	4	5
M. Other _____	1	2	3	4	5

PLEASE PROCEED TO QUESTION 12

12) Which of the following best describes your organization?

__ A. Corporation or business

__ B. Economic, trade, or professional association

__ C. Labor union

__ D. Citizens association or public interest group

__ E. Other (please specify) _____

13) Please indicate your organization's total revenue for the last fiscal year.
$_____

14) What percent of your organization's total revenue is spent on political activities in a typical year? _____%

PLEASE ANSWER QUESTIONS 15–17 ONLY IF YOUR ORGANIZATION IS A **VOLUNTARY ASSOCIATION** (economic assn., trade assn., professional assn., labor union, citizens assn., or public interest group).

15) Some organizations are composed of other organizations or representatives of organizations, such as companies, institutions, or associations, while other organizations are made up only of individuals representing themselves. Still other organizations have a membership that includes a mixture of organizations or organizational representatives and individuals. Which membership category best describes your organization?

   __ A. Organizations or organizational representatives

   __ B. A mixture of organizations or organizational representatives and
        individuals

   __ C. Individuals

16) What is the total membership of your organization?

   ____ # individual members

   ____ # organizations or organizational representatives

17) Organizations receive financial support from a variety of sources. Please indicate your best estimate of the percentage that each source contributes to your organization.

   ____ A. Membership dues

   ____ B. Revenues from advertising

   ____ C. Conventions and/or conferences

   ____ D. Sale of merchandise

   ____ E. Grants from government agencies

   ____ F. Gifts or donations from businesses or corporations

   ____ G. Gifts or donations from individuals (not membership dues)

   ____ H. Gifts or transfers from other organizations

   ____ I. Loans

   ____ J. Other (please specify) _____

18) Approximately how long did it take you to complete this survey? ____ minutes

Please return the completed survey to:

Professor Elisabeth Gerber
Department of Political Science
University of California, San Diego
La Jolla, CA 92093-0521
(619) 534-2022 Phone
(619) 822-0564 Fax

THANK YOU FOR YOUR PARTICIPATION.

References

Ashford, Kathryn L. 1986. "The Role of Corporations in the 1980 Congressional Elections." *Sociological Inquiry* 56:409–31.

Barber, Mary Beth. 1993. "Compromising on CEQA." *California Journal* October: 35–37.

Bentley, Arthur F. 1967. *The Process of Government*, ed. Peter H. Odegard. Cambridge, Mass.: Belknap Press of Harvard University Press.

Berry, Jeffrey M. 1977. *Lobbying for the People*. Princeton, N.J.: Princeton University Press.

Bowler, Shaun, and Todd Donovan. 1998. *Demanding Choices: Opinion, Voting and Direct Democracy*. Ann Arbor: University of Michigan Press.

Butler, David, and Austin Ranney. 1994. *Referendums Around the World: The Growing Use of Direct Democracy*. Washington, D.C.: AEI Press.

California Bill Tracking Statenet. 1997. (Lexis, Statetrack, Bill).

California Commission on Campaign Financing. 1992. *Democracy by Initiative: Shaping California's Fourth Branch of Government*. Los Angeles: Center for Responsive Government.

California Fair Political Practices Commission. 1988a. "Summary of Receipts and Expenditures by Committees Primarily Formed to Qualify, Support, or Oppose a State Ballot Measure." 1988 Primary Election. Sacramento, Calif.

———. 1988b. "Summary of Receipts and Expenditures by Committees Primarily Formed to Qualify, Support, or Oppose a State Ballot Measure." 1988 General Election. Sacramento, Calif.

———. 1990a. "Summary of Receipts and Expenditures by Committees Primarily Formed to Qualify, Support, or Oppose a State Ballot Measure." 1990 Primary Election. Sacramento, Calif.

———. 1990b. "Summary of Receipts and Expenditures by Committees Primarily Formed to Qualify, Support, or Oppose a State Ballot Measure." 1990 General Election. Sacramento, Calif.

California Secretary of State. 1994a. "Statement of the Vote, General Election." November. Sacramento, Calif.

———. 1994b. "Campaign Receipts and Expenditures." Sacramento, Calif.

———. 1996. "Campaign Receipts and Expenditures." Sacramento, Calif.

Chappell, Henry W., Jr. 1981. "Campaign Contributions and Voting on the Cargo Preference Bill: A Comparison of Simultaneous Models." *Public Choice* 36:301–12.

———. 1982. "Campaign Contributions and Congressional Voting: A Simultaneous Probit-Tobit Model." *Review of Economics and Statistics* 62:77–83.

Coughlin, Cletus G. 1985. "Domestic Content Legislation: House Voting and the Economic Theory of Regulation." *Economic Inquiry* 23:437–48.

Council of State Governments. 1991, 1992, 1996. *The Book of the States*. Lexington, Ky.: Council of State Governments.

Crawford, Vincent, and Joel Sobel. 1982. "Strategic Information Transmission." *Econometrica* 50:1431–51.

Cronin, Thomas E. 1989. *Direct Democracy: The Politics of Initiative, Referendum, and Recall.* Cambridge, Mass.: Harvard University Press.

Dahl, Robert A. 1961. *Who Governs?* New Haven, Conn.: Yale University Press.

Deverell, William, and Tom Sitton. 1994. *California Progressivism Revisited.* Berkeley: University of California Press.

DiCamillo, Mark, and Mervin Field. 1990–1996. "The Field Poll." Release dates 1990–1996. San Francisco: The Field Institute.

Dubin, Jeffrey A., D. Roderick Kiewiet, and Charles Noussair. 1992. "Voting on Growth Control Measures: Preferences and Strategies." *Economics and Politics* 4:191–213.

Dubois, Philip L., and Floyd F. Feeney. 1992. *Improving the California Initiative Process: Options for Change.* Berkeley: California Policy Seminar, University of California.

Durden, Garey C., Jason F. Shogren, and Jonathan I. Siberman. 1991. "The Effects of Interest Group Pressure on Coal Strip-Mining Legislation." *Social Science Quarterly* 72:237–50.

Elkins, Stanley, and Eric McKitrick. 1993. *The Age of Federalism.* New York: Oxford University Press.

Erikson, Robert S., and Gerald C. Wright. 1993. "Voters, Candidates, and Issues in Congressional Elections." In *Congress Reconsidered*, 5th ed., ed. Lawrence C. Dodd and Bruce I. Oppenheimer, 91–115. Washington, D.C.: CQ Press.

Erikson, Robert S., Gerald C. Wright, and John P. McIver. 1993. *Statehouse Democracy: Public Opinion and Policy in the American States.* Cambridge: Cambridge University Press.

Feldstein, Paul J., and Glenn Melnick. 1984. "Congressional Voting Behavior on Hospital Legislation: An Exploratory Study." *Journal of Health Politics, Policy and Law* 8:686–701.

Fenno, Richard F. 1978. *Home Style: House Members in Their Districts.* Boston: Little, Brown.

Ferejohn, John. 1974. *Pork Barrel Politics: Rivers and Harbors Legislation, 1947–1968.* Stanford, Calif.: Stanford University Press.

Fleisher, Richard. 1993. "PAC Contributions and Congressional Voting on National Defense." *Legislative Studies Quarterly* 18:391–409.

Fowler, Linda L., and Ronald G. Shaiko. 1987. "The Grass Roots Connection: Environmental Activists and Senate Roll Calls." *American Journal of Political Science* 31:484–510.

Gerber, Elisabeth R. 1996. "Legislative Response to the Threat of Popular Initiatives." *American Journal of Political Science* 40:99–128.

Gerber, Elisabeth R., and John E. Jackson. 1993. "Endogenous Preferences and the Study of Institutions." *American Political Science Review* 87: 639–56.

Gerber, Elisabeth R., and Arthur Lupia. 1995. "Campaign Competition and Policy Responsiveness in Direct Legislation Elections." *Political Behavior* 17:287–306.

———. 1998. "Voter Competence in Direct Legislation Elections." In *Citizen Competence*, ed. Steven Elkins and Karol Soltan. University Park, Pa.: Pennsylvania State University Press.

Ginsberg, Benjamin, and John C. Green. 1986. "The Best Congress Money Can Buy:

Campaign Contributions and Congressional Behavior." In *Do Elections Matter?*, ed. Benjamin Ginsberg and Alan Stone. Armonk, N.Y.: M. E. Sharpe.

Gray, Virginia, and David Lowery. 1996. *The Population Ecology of Interest Representation*. Ann Arbor: University of Michigan Press.

Grenzke, Janet M. 1989a. "PACs and the Congressional Supermarket: The Currency Is Complex." *American Journal of Political Science* 33:1–24.

———. 1989b. "Candidate Attributes and PAC Contributions." *Western Political Quarterly* 42:245–64.

Hahn, Harlan, and Sheldon Kamieniecki. 1987. *Referendum Voting: Social Status and Policy Preferences*. Westport, Conn.: Greenwood Press.

Hamilton, Alexander, James Madison, and John Jay. 1961. *The Federalist Papers*, ed. Clinton Rossiter, New York: Mentor.

Henshaw, Stanley K., and Jennifer Van Vort. 1994. "Abortion Services in the United States, 1991 and 1992." *Family Planning Perspectives* 26:3.

Idaho Secretary of State. 1988, 1992. "Contributions to Committees Supporting or Opposing a Statewide Measure." Boise, Idaho.

Jackson, John E. 1989. "An Errors-in-Variables Approach to Estimating Models with Small Area Data." *Political Analysis* 1:157–80.

Jones, Woodrow, Jr., and K. Robert Keiser. 1987. "Issue Visibility and the Effects of PAC Money." *Social Science Quarterly* 68:170–76.

Kabashima, Ikuo, and Hideo Sato. 1986. "Local Content and Congressional Politics: Interest Group Theory and Foreign Policy Implications." *International Studies Quarterly* 30:295–314.

Kalt, Joseph P., and Mark A. Zupan. 1984. "Capture and Ideology in the Economic Theory of Politics." *American Economic Review* 74:279–99.

Kenny, Lawrence W., and Rebecca B. Morton. 1993. "Representation, Parties, and Policy Divergence in the U.S. Senate." Working Paper, Department of Political Science, University of Iowa, Iowa City.

King, David C. and Jack L. Walker, Jr. 1991. "An Ecology of Interest Groups in America." In *Mobilizing Interest Groups in America*, ed. Jack L. Walker, Jr. Ann Arbor: University of Michigan Press.

Kingdon, John W. 1989. *Congressmen's Voting Decisions*. 3d ed. Ann Arbor: University of Michigan Press.

Kollman, Ken. 1998. *Outside Lobbying: Public Opinion and Interest Group Strategies*. Princeton, N.J.: Princeton University Press.

Langbein, Laura I., and Mark A. Lotwis. 1990. "The Political Efficacy of Lobbying and Money: Gun Control in the U.S. House, 1986." *Legislative Studies Quarterly* 15:413–40.

Los Angeles Times. 1988. "Changing the Petition Rules." Friday, 16 February, metro edition, part 2, p. 6.

Lowenstein, Daniel. 1982. "Campaign Spending and Ballot Propositions: Recent Experience, Public Choice Theory, and the First Amendment." *UCLA Law Review* 29:505–641.

Lowi, Theodore J. 1969. *The End of Liberalism*. New York: Norton.

———. 1972. "Four Systems of Policy, Politics, and Choice." *Public Administration Review* 32:298–310.

Lupia, Arthur. 1992. "Busy Voters, Agenda Control, and the Power of Information." *American Political Science Review* 86:390–403.

———. 1994. "Shortcuts versus Encyclopedias: Information and Voting Behavior in California Insurance Reform Elections." *American Political Science Review* 88:63–76.

———. 1997. "Who Can Persuade Whom? How Simple Cues Affect Political Attitudes." Working Paper. University of California, San Diego.

Lupia, Arthur, and Mathew D. McCubbins. 1998. *The Democratic Dilemma: Can Citizens Learn What They Need to Know?* New York: Cambridge University Press.

Magleby, David B. 1984. *Direct Legislation: Voting on Ballot Propositions in the United States.* Baltimore: Johns Hopkins University Press.

Masters, Marick F., and Asghar Zardkoohi. 1988. "Congressional Support for Unions' Positions across Diverse Legislation." *Journal of Labor Research* 9:149–65.

Matsusaka, John G. 1995. "Fiscal Effects of the Voter Initiative: Evidence from the Last 30 Years." *Journal of Political Economy* 103: 587–623.

McArthur, John, and Steven V. Marks. 1988. "Constituent Interest vs. Legislator Ideology: The Role of Political Opportunity Cost." *Economic Inquiry* July:461–70.

McConnell, Grant. 1966. *Private Power and American Democracy.* New York: Alfred A. Knopf.

Michigan Secretary of State. 1988, 1992. "Expenditures by Ballot Question Committees." Lansing, Mich.

Miller, Warren E., Donald R. Kinder, Steven J. Rosenstone, and the National Election Studies. 1993. *American National Election Study: Pooled Senate Election Study, 1988, 1990, 1992* [computer file]. 2d release. Ann Arbor: University of Michigan, Center for Political Studies [producer], 1993. Ann Arbor: Inter-University Consortium for Political and Social Research [distributor], 1993.

Missouri Secretary of State. 1988–1992. "Missouri Annual Campaign Finance Report." Jefferson City, Mo.

NARAL Foundation/NARAL. 1991, 1993, 1998. *Who Decides: A State-by-State Review of Abortion Rights.* Washington, D.C.: NARAL.

Nebraska Accountability and Disclosure Commission. 1988, 1990, 1992. "A Summary of Political Campaign Financing." Lincoln, Neb.

Olson, Mancur. 1965. *The Logic of Collective Action.* Cambridge, Mass.: Harvard University Press.

Oregon Secretary of State, Elections Division. 1988, 1990, 1992. "Summary Report of Campaign Contributions and Expenditures." Salem, Oreg.

Owens, John E. 1986. "The Impact of Campaign Contributions on Legislative Outcomes in Congress: Evidence from a House Committee." *Political Studies* 34:285–95.

Owens, John R., and Larry L. Wade. 1986. "Campaign Spending on California Ballot Propositions, Trends and Effects, 1924–1984." *Western Political Quarterly* 36:675–89.

Peltzman, Sam. 1984. "Constituent Interest and Congressional Voting." *Journal of Law and Economics* 27:181–210.

Public Affairs Research Institute of New Jersey. 1992. *Initiative and Referendum Analysis* 2:1–15.

Radwin, David. 1996. "The Electoral Advantages of Candidate-Sponsored Initiatives."

Senior Honors Thesis, Department of Political Science, University of California, San Diego.

Roberts, Jerry. 1994. "Hiram Johnson, Please Call Home." *San Francisco Chronicle*, Saturday, 10 September, sec. editorial, p. A20.

Romer, Thomas, and Howard Rosenthal. 1978. "Political Resource Allocation, Controlled Agendas, and the Status Quo." *Public Choice* 33:27–44.

Rothenberg, Lawrence S. 1992. *Linking Citizens to Government: Interest Group Politics at Common Cause*. New York: Cambridge, University Press.

Salisbury, Robert H. 1969. "An Exchange Theory of Interest Groups." *Midwest Journal of Political Science* 13:1–32.

———. 1984. "Interest Representation: The Dominance of Institutions." *American Political Science Review* 78:64–76.

Saltzman, Gregory M. 1987. "Congressional Voting Labor Issues: The Role of PACs." *Industrial and Labor Relations Review* 40:163–79.

Schattschneider, E. E. 1960. *The Semi-Sovereign People*. New York: Holt, Rinehart and Winston.

Schlozman, Kay Lehman. 1984. "What Accent the Heavenly Chorus? Political Equality and the American Pressure System." *Journal of Politics* 46:1006–32.

Schlozman, Kay Lehman, and John T. Tierney. 1986. *Organized Interests and American Democracy*. New York: Harper and Row.

Schrag, Peter. 1998. *Paradise Lost*. New York: The New Press.

Sears, David O., and Jack Citrin. 1985. *Tax Revolt: Something for Nothing in California*. Cambridge, Mass.: Harvard University Press.

Segal, Jeffrey A., Charles M. Cameron, and Albert D. Cover. 1992. "A Spatial Model of Roll Call Voting: Senators, Constituents, Presidents, and Interest Groups in Supreme Court Confirmations." *American Journal of Political Science* 36:96–121.

Shepsle, Kenneth, and Barry Weingast. 1987. "The Institutional Foundations of Committee Power." *American Political Science Review* 81:85–104.

Shuit, Douglas, and Kenneth Reich. 1988. "$130 Million Spent on Ballot Issues; $76 Million Contributed in Fight over 5 Insurance Initiatives Alone." *Los Angeles Times*, Friday, 4 November, sec. 1, p. 1.

Silberman, Jonathan I., and Garey Durden. 1976. "Determining Legislature Preferences on the Minimum Wage: An Economic Approach." *Journal of Political Economy* 36:96–121.

Smith, Richard A. 1984. "Advocacy, Interpretation and Influence in the U.S. Congress." *American Political Science Review* 78:44–63.

———. 1993. "Agreement, Defection, and Interest-Group Influence in the U.S. Congress." In *Agenda Formation*, ed. William H. Riker. Ann Arbor: University of Michigan Press.

———. 1995. "Interest Group Influence in the U.S. Congress." *Legislative Studies Quarterly* 20:89–139.

Spence, Michael. 1973. "Job Market Signaling." *Quarterly Journal of Economics* 87:355–74.

Squire, Peverill. 1992. "Legislative Professionalism and Membership Diversity in State Legislatures." *Legislative Studies Quarterly* 19:69–79.

State of Maine, Committee on Governmental Ethics and Election Practices. 1989–1991. "PAC Report Form," individual campaign committees. Augusta, Maine.

Stratmann, Thomas. 1991. "What Do Campaign Contributions Buy? Deciphering Causal Effects of Money and Votes." *Southern Economic Journal* 57:606–20.

Thomas, Clive S., and Ronald J. Hrebenar. 1996. "Interest Groups in the States." In *Politics in the American States: A Comparative Analysis.* 6th ed., ed. Virginia Gray, Herbert Jacob, and Kenneth Vines. Boston: Little, Brown.

Truman, David B. 1951. *The Governmental Process: Political Interests and Public Opinion.* New York: Alfred A. Knopf.

U.S. Department of Commerce. 1991. *Statistical Abstract of the United States.* 111th ed. Washington: Bureau of the Census.

———. 1995. *Statistical Abstract of the United States.* 115th ed. Washington: Bureau of the Census.

———. 1998. Bureau of the Census Internet site. http://www.census.gov/ftp/pubs/govs/www/index.html.

U.S. Department of Justice. 1996. *Capital Punishment 1994.* Washington: Bureau of Justice Statistics.

Vesenka, Mary H. 1989. "Economic Interests and Ideological Conviction: A Note on PACs and Agriculture Acts." *Journal of Economic Behavior and Organization* 12:259–63.

Walker, Jack L. 1969. "The Diffusion of Innovations among the American States." *American Political Science Review* 63:880–99.

———. 1991. *Mobilizing Interest Groups in America: Patrons, Professions, and Social Movements.* Ann Arbor: University of Michigan Press.

Washington Secretary of State. 1988–1994. "Bank Deposits and Cash Receipts" records, individual campaign committees. Olympia, Wash.

Welch, William P. 1982. "Campaign Contributions and Legislative Voting: Milk Money and Dairy Price Supports." *Western Political Quarterly* 35:478–95.

Wilhite, Allen, and John Theilmann. 1987. "Labor PAC Contributions and Labor Legislation: A Simultaneous Logit Approach." *Public Choice* 53:267–76.

Wilson, James Q. 1974. *Political Organizations.* New York: Basic Books.

Wright, John R. 1985. "PACs, Contributions, and Roll Calls: An Organizational Perspective." *American Political Science Review* 79:400–414.

———. 1990. "Contributions, Lobbying, and Committee Voting in the U.S. House of Representatives." *American Political Science Review* 84:417–38.

Index

AB 544, 24
abortion policy, 16, 54, 66
abortion rate, 123–25
absentee ballots, 42
access to state legislators, 139, 143
advisory propositions, 15
Aerospace Industries, 67
affirmative action, 53, 121
AFL-CIO, 26
agenda setting, 44, 45n, 48, 55
agrarian interests, 4
Air Transport Association of America, 69
Alaska, provisions for direct legislation in, 16n
alcohol tax, 15n
American Civil Liberties Union, 69
American Hospital Association, 67
Arizona, provisions for direct legislation in, 44n
Association of American Medical Colleges, 67
Atlantic Richfield Co., 70
Australia, usage of direct legislation in, 15–16
autonomous individuals, 8; definition of, 66

ballot order, 41, 61
ballot pamphlet, 145
ballot placement, 42
behavioral hurdles, 77; definition of, 52
Bentley, Arthur, 12
Berry, Jeffrey, 14
binding propositions, 15
Bowler, Shaun, 57, 145
Buckley v. Valeo, 43
business and labor regulation, 104
businesses, coding of, 78
Butler, David, 16

California Beer and Wine Wholesalers Association, 69
California: disclosure requirements in, 77n; inclusion of, in survey, 77; insurance initiatives in, 53, 145; measures of, in sample, 79n; provisions for legislative amendments in, 44; postelection amendability in, 137;

signature requirement in, 40; usage of direct legislation in, 16, 80
California Environmental Quality Act, 24
California Nurses Association, 26
California Optometric Association, 70
California Taxpayers Association, 70
California Trial Lawyers Association, 70
Californians against Unfair Rate Increases No on Prop 100 and 103, 78n, 98n
campaign ads, 64
campaign committees, 41; contributing to, 46, 49, 52; formation of, 45–46, 49
campaign contributions, 4, 13, 63; from citizen interests, 95; from economic interests, 95
campaign costs, 80
campaign finance laws, 21, 61, 121
Canada, usage of direct legislation in, 15–16
candidate contributors, coding of, 78
capital punishment, 54. *See also* death penalty
change-oriented preferences and citizen interest groups, 10
channels of communication, 17
charter school regulation, 24
checks and balances, 143
Chevron Corporation, 70
cigarette and tobacco tax, 15n
circulation period, 40, 60
citizen interest groups: and autonomous individuals, 68; coding of, 78; comparative advantages of, 70; examples of, 69; King and Walker definition of, 67
citizen interests: categorization of, 102; motivations of, 104
Citizens Against Red Tape, 24
Citizens against Rent Control v. City of Berkeley, 43
Citizens for No Fault Sponsored by CA Insurers, 98n
Citrin, Jack, 121, 143
civil laws, 16
collective action problem, 11n, 65, 144; external, 65; internal, 65
Committee for Fair Lawyers Fees Sponsored by Insurance Industries, 98n